The Real McCoy:
The Story of a Creek and Its Town

Copyright © 1975 Norma Stevens
Reprinted in Facsimile Edition 2010 by Jolibro Publishing

All rights reserved.
No part of this book may be used or reproduced, or stored in a retrieval system, or transmitted in any form or by any means, electronic, mechanical, photocopying, recording, or otherwise, without written permission of the publisher, except in the case of brief quotations embodied in critical articles and reviews.

For permissions, group sales, wholesale purchases, or other matters pertaining to this work, contact Jolibro Publishing, info@jolibro.com

Visit our Facebook page for "The Real McCoy Book" at
www.facebook.com/RealMcCoyBook

Cover Art Credits:
Front cover photo: "Bridge Far," copyright © 2010 by Shelley Morgan O'Bryant.
Front cover inset: Oil painting of the Bainton Mill by Mrs. Charles (Amy) Bainton, courtesy of the Bainton family.
Back cover painting: "The Spirit of McCoy's Creek," copyright © 2010 by Toni Lacey-Verdon.
Back cover inset: High school graduation photo of the author, Norma Stevens (1922–2008).

ISBN 978-0-0924691-2-5
Library of Congress Control Number 2010929441

Subject keywords:
Michigan history; Buchanan, Michigan; Berrien County; Native American history; McCoy's Creek; water power; Potawatomie; Ottawa; Chief Pokagon; Chief Moccasin; Chief Topinabee; Land of the Four Flags; Isaac McCoy; Charles Cowles; Clark Equipment Company; Norma Stevens

Jolibro Publishing
www.jolibro.com

THE REAL McCOY

The Story of a Creek and Its Town

by
Norma Stevens

Printed and Published 1975 by Record Publishing Company

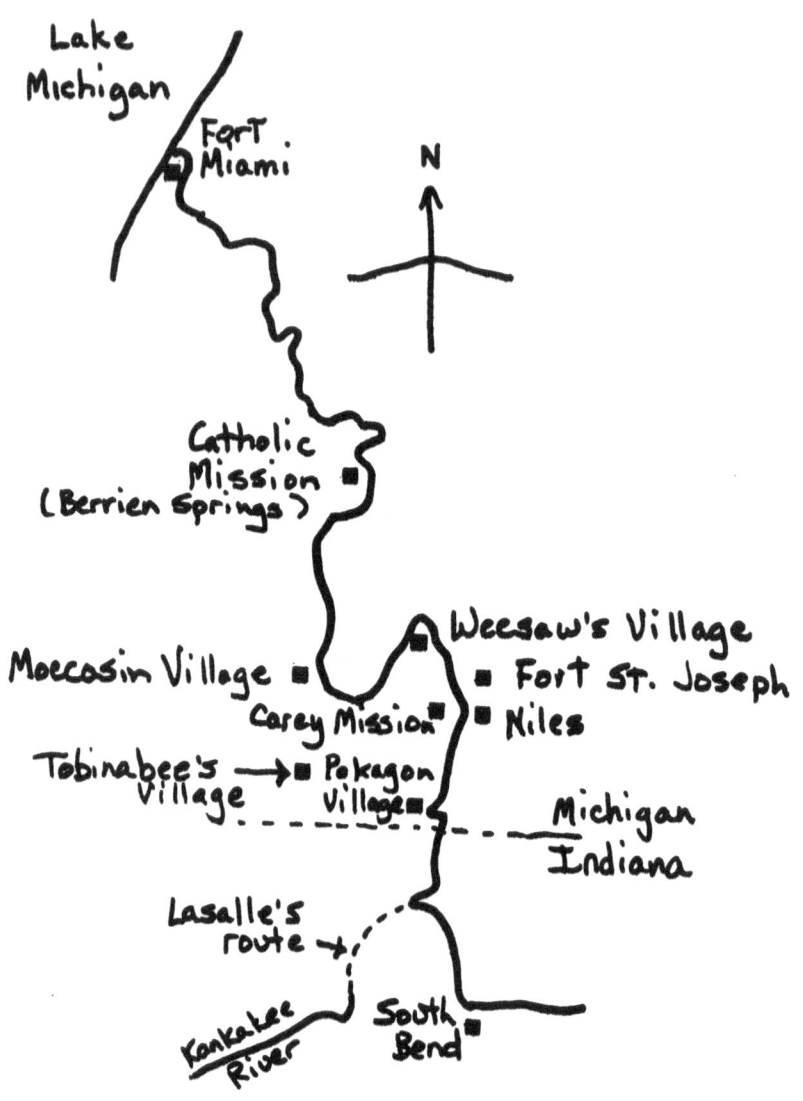

Copyright, 1975
by Norma Stevens

THE BAINTON MILL... This is a reproduction of a large oil painting made around the turn of the century by Mrs. Charles (Amy) Bainton, mother of Kelsey Bainton. Viewed from the downstream, or eastern side, of the mill, the painting depicts the system used to increase the water power to the mill, with the small structures in the right foreground housing the pulley assemblies from the lower dam to the mill. This painting is also reproduced on the cover of this book, courtesy of the Bainton family.

Foreword

THE REAL McCOY

A Story of a Creek and Its Town

   This story began with a daydream. An intermittent, persistent daydream which I prefer not to call loafing on the job but which nevertheless developed during my several years as a reporter at the Berrien County Record. From my desk in the Record office I had, for some years, a clear view across Days Avenue to the waterfall at the Buchanan Co-ops mill, and my eyes would be frequently drawn to this magnetic, perpetual rush of water, plunging from a great culvert down into a stone-walled sluiceway, only to disappear again beneath the streets, hurrying to join the St. Joseph River, bound for an inland sea.
   Because I had access to the big books holding copies of past issues of the paper through all the years ("the morgue", it's called in newspaper jargon) I found, during that time, many fascinating news stories of the past relating to McCoy's Creek, and soon became aware of this stream's vital part in our local history. It was obvious that the power potential of McCoy's Creek had been the magnet that first drew the westward-moving pioneers to its banks. This little brook had given birth to the town!
   As I pored over those yellowed pages in the back room at the Record, I realized that others were as ignorant of the town's heritage as I had been; and I would look again at the waterfalls across the way and picture the past glories of this lusty stream, Nature's gift to this valley which, like Alfred Tennyson's brook, goes on and on forever...though now unused and nearly unnoticed.
   Then one day in the mid-1960's, heavy earth-moving equipment appeared and began the job of forcing the water below the millrace into still more huge culverts; and within a few months there was at that site a fine new office building and a parking lot. No longer able to see the falls from "my" window, I would then sometimes put a sandwich in my pocket and go find a grassy bank where strangers were still allowed to venture; and eventually my daydreams deepened into an inward cry of frustration and urgency:
   Some words should be said for this McCoy's Creek! Some memories stirred...some approbation given...some hope dredged up for its reprieve...or, at least, some requiem offered.
   And so, during one of my several "retirements" from the newspaper, the first research work for this history was begun. The original plan was to write only a brief history of the creek itself, but I soon discovered that the history of McCoy's Creek and of Buchanan were so inseparably interwoven that they must be told as one. I must confess that, had I known then that this work would develop into a booklength chronicle, I'm sure I should never have had the courage to begin.
   However, many local persons gave invaluable assistance in this history by making available family records, books, photographs, and their own

recollections. I am especially grateful to Mr. and Mrs. Kelsey Bainton, who provided not only valuable material but also many hours of their time for interviews. My heartfelt thanks to Mrs. Clarence Hartline, a dedicated local historian; also former librarian Mrs. Claude Lauver, the family of the late Mrs. Bert Mitchell, Mr. Frank Habicht, Mrs. Kenneth Huston, and many other individuals who have offered assistance and the use of pictures.

In addition to past volumes of the Berrien County Record, research sources for this book have included: "A Twentieth Century History of Berrien County" by Judge Orville W. Coolidge, published 1906; "Berrien County History and Directory", by Edward Cowles, published in Buchanan, 1871, by Record Steam Printing Company; "Atlas of Berrien County, Michigan" by C.O. Titus, published 1873; "Atlas of Berrien County, Michigan", by W.W. Graves, published 1887; "The Michigan Wallins", by Van A. Wallin, published 1933; Ensign's "History of Berrien and Van Buren Counties", published 1880; "Land of the Four Flags", by Wilbur M. Cunningham, published 1961.

The reader is asked to indulge this writer in some words of very special indebtedness.

Much inspiration for this story...indeed for pursuing the delights and wretchedness of writing itself...has come from the enkindling influence of the late Walter Hawes, editor of the Berrien County Record for 27 years. This gentle, shy poet with a melancholy-to-rollicking spirit...totally devoted to his adopted town, served Buchanan as humanist, humorist, and historian through his newspaper writing for much of his lifetime. In my girlhood, he had been an acquaintance, an admirable veteran of the "fourth estate", an occasional tutor to an aspiring journalist. In death, he became a dear friend through the legacy of his words upon the printed page.

Many of the anecdotes and much historical reference material for this work were adapted from Mr. Hawes' columns, "Tales of an Old Town", "The Story of Buchanan", "Now Here's the Proposition", and "With the Medal Men at Clark's", all of which appeared for many years in the local newspaper. Additional material was gained through Letters to the Editor, inspired by the Hawes columns, often written by "old-timers" now no longer with us to tell us of the past.

It now occurs to me that a Foreword in a book such as this affords the author a one-and-only chance to make excuses and apologies for the failures and omissions that are about to be revealed. Therefore, I add the following:

Because this history was originally written for publication in the Berrien County Record (where it appeared as a feature series in 1967), source references and footnotes were not included throughout; and it was then impossible to annotate the work in rewriting and editing the story to appear in book form.

Although essential facts and dates and significant events are included, with much research and cross-checking to assure accuracy in so far as possible, the writer did attempt to especially emphasize the overall picture of the life of the people through the decades, and to reconstruct the moods and tenor of the changing community.

Richard Whately once wrote, "Historians give us the extraordinary events, and omit just what we want, the every-day life of each particular time and country."

"The Real McCoy", then, is offered as a narrative history. It is hoped that the serious student of history will find in these pages enough detailed information to be of research value, and that the casual reader will find herein an easy, readable story that will enable him vicariously to hear the creak of water wheel and gears, to smell the fresh sawdust and the sweet flour aroma of a dozen mills, to sense the drama of good times and bad in a fledgling community, and to see in the mind's eye the people and environs of "those good old days".

N.S.

THE FISHING WAS GOOD . . . Lumber and other debris near the dam mar this picture of a lone fisherman in downtown Buchanan. The scene was photographed behind the present Dan's Rexall Drugs, where a city parking lot is now located. The caption on the photo says, "Old Dam, 1913 on McCoy's Creek, known as the Kinger and Marble Mills."

> "The Lord, thy God, bringeth thee into a good land,
> a land of brooks, of water, of fountains and depths that
> spring out of valleys and hills" ..... The Bible

Chapter One

THE BECKONING WATERS

It begins in the swamplands west and south of Buchanan where Nature...sometimes shy about such wonders...has hidden the fountainhead springs behind tangles of ironwood, wild huckleberry, sandbar willow, and wild flag.

Here, in basins once sculptured and fed by the melting, receding glaciers of an ancient age...in black, shaky bogs that have defied the drying suns and winds of centuries...the perpetual waters continue to arise and scramble to seek their kind, running together in rivulets to form the first fragile fingers of a stream. Joined by many more springs along shallow banks, the headwaters rush along in gathering strength in a winding, downhill run from the western edges of Bertrand Township...finally to spill out, some seven miles below, into the mightier current of the St. Joseph River.

Thus have the ebullient waters of McCoy's Creek for untold centuries coursed through this valley in southwestern Michigan.

McCoy's Creek is not a large stream...in fact, when located on a map and compared with the overall topography of our "water wonderland" state, it seems quite insignificant, yet, were there no McCoy's Creek here, it is likely there would be no Buchanan, nor a town of any name, in this place. The brief, bright stream with a name like a prizefighter's has fulfilled a maternal destiny in giving birth to, and nurturing, a small settlement which matured into the City of Buchanan within the span of a century.

To tell the story, one is of course expected to begin at the beginning; and so, at the very outset, we are confounded, for how can we really know when or how our story began? We can only follow the theories and reconstructions of geologists, who tell us that at some time, during eons unknown, the waters of the St. Joseph River, which originally flowed southward toward the Mississippi, were by some mysterious force turned northward (at South Bend) to forge a new course through a new valley into Lake Michigan. Scientists believe that Lake Michigan and the other Great Lakes were gouged out between 20,000 and 100,000 years ago as the Labrador ice sheet advanced and withdrew during the last glacial epoch, and that the melting ice left behind hundreds of smaller lakes and streams...some to dry up during the intervening thousands of years, and many more remaining to mark lavishly in blue the present-day maps of Minnesota, Wisconsin, and Michigan.

Following the upheavals of the earth caused by these mighty ice sheets (some estimated to have been 2,500 feet thick in this area) it can be assumed that the embryonic springs of our own little creek one day arose from the newly created swamplands to the west and sent their clear waters sluicing eastward through a lovely valley to the river.

Let us then expand our imaginations to picture the moving creatures who lived here during the Ice Age and after...the giant beaver, mastodon, mammoth, great moose...and early man, before whose crude spears the last remaining prehistoric animals finally faltered and died.

The aborigines of our territory...the Sandia Man, Folsom Man, the Mound Builders...were succeeded in the following centuries, through evolution and migration, by primitive Indian tribes, and later by advanced bands of Wyandottes, Chippewas, Miamis, and at last the Potawatomies, who roamed and camped over great areas and finally made these lands their home.

Here, at last, with the coming of the Potawatomies to the St. Joseph River Valley, our story of McCoy's Creek has its firm beginnings.

Through the legends and stories of the Indians themselves, we know of Indian hunters seeking wild duck and turkeys in the McCoy's Creek headlands...of their spearing huge sturgeon and trout in the shallow riffles along its length... trapping the muskrat, otter, and beaver...stalking with bow and arrow the deer and bear.

Soon familiar trails and crossing places were beaten into the banks of the creek by the tread of many moccasined feet; and at last the women of Chief Moccasin's village to the north and the village of Mishaquaka to the south ventured up and down the stream to gather wild berries, dig roots, and cut rushes for weaving into baskets and mats.

For some time preceding the close of the 18th century, the Potawatomies were the sole occupants of the St. Joseph Valley; and they enjoyed exclusive rights to all the waters, the lands, and the many provisions of nature in which the land was so bountifully endowed. These they reportedly exchanged freely, in shared friendship and brotherhood, with the Ottawa tribes of eastern Michigan.

Their peaceful, pastoral existence in the great valley was to be numbered in short decades, however.

First White Explorers

Here we must go back in time 250 years, for, as early as the mid-1600's, the white man had already made his first appearance in the area with the invasion of sharp-eyed runners for the French merchants of Quebec and Montreal who were engaged in the fur trade.

Before long, the country was visited by the French explorers and Catholic missionaries whose names are familiar to students of history...Father Marquette, LaSalle, Charlevoix, Father Allouez, and others.

In 1666, Father Allouez, whose grave is believed to be located beneath a marker in the south part of Niles, wrote in his journal about the people he found in this area, "The Potawatomies are a people whose country is about the lake Ill-i-mouch (Michigan). They are a warlike people, hunters and fishers. Their country is good for Indian corn, of which they plant many fields. Of all the people that I have associated with in these countries, they are the most docile and affectionate towards the French."

Around 1800, villages of Potawatomies were scattered throughout the Niles-Buchanan area. Chief "Cog" (sometimes known as Kawk or "Porcupine") Moccasin ruled the largest village in what would one day become the Buchanan area, consisting of about 300 inhabitants. The village of Mishaquaka was two miles south; and there were smaller villages along the river and scattered here and there to the south and the west. A heavily traveled trail followed the south bank of the river in what is now the Bend of the River area from Chief Moccasin's village north of Buchanan to Chief Weesaw's village northwest of Niles at a point where the river turns again, sharply southward, towards Niles. Chiefs Topinabee and Pokagon were quartered south and west of Niles.

In this story, whose purpose is to explore the history of McCoy's Creek and the growth of Buchanan, we shall not dwell upon that intricate part of our history dealing with the long struggle for possession of the land by the French, English, and Spanish.

Because of its nearness to our community and its prominence in local history, however, some mention should be made of Fort St. Joseph at Niles. This military post was established by the French in 1691 at a point about one mile south of Niles on the west bank of the St. Joseph River. The fort, along with nearby missions and a trading post, was to become the most important station in southwestern Michigan during the years of the white man's conquest of America. The great Sauk Trail from Detroit to Chicago (later known as Chicago Road) passed through Bertrand a short distance south of the fort; and the area was criss-crossed with lesser trails.

In 1761, Fort St. Joseph was taken over by the British, after war with the French over American territories. In 1763, a treaty was signed, giving England all the territory east of the Mississippi; and in that same year Fort St. Joseph was captured by a small band of Potawatomies on orders from Chief Pontiac at Detroit, and held for a year before being returned to the British.

In 1781, a Spanish force from St. Louis marched 400 miles northward, captured Fort St. Joseph, raised the Spanish flag, stayed a few days, and then burned down the fort before returning to their main garrison. In 1796, thirteen years after the British officially relinquished the land, the British flag came down and the fourth national flag, Old Glory, was at last raised over what was left of the fort.

The reader will have now noticed that this writer has just disposed of two centuries of basic American history...including the Revolutionary War and the War of 1812...in three paragraphs. (History teachers, have mercy!) Truly, many consequential and fascinating details of those years as they affected the history of the St. Joseph Valley are well worth further study; and the serious student is urged to supplement his reading by making use of the fine volumes to be found in the local history section of the Buchanan Public Library and other nearby libraries.

Our chosen task here is rather to extract and dissect just one tiny kernel from the swelling, proliferating seed pod of American history...our own McCoy's Creek and its environs.

Chapter Two

ISAAC McCOY, SHEPHERD OF THE WILDERNESS

During the early years of the 19th century, the Potawatomies of this area, although ostensibly protected by treaty and by their reserved lands here, were already being pressured and intimidated by the invading white man.

They found fresh hope and inspiration...however briefly...in the appearance of a new kind of missionary on the scene, the Rev. Isaac McCoy.

The Rev. McCoy, a Baptist clergyman, had by the year 1823 negotiated with the Indians and the government a consignment of a mile-square section of land west of Niles, had established a thriving mission on the site, and started a school attended by 30 Indian children. The Carey Mission (named for a famous Baptist missionary then stationed in Hindustan) was so successful in fact, that it was to have an almost immediate bearing on the settlement and prosperity of the St. Joseph River Valley, and thereby ironically led to the final defeat of the very Indians Rev. McCoy had come to help.

In 1820, Rev. McCoy had established a school and mission at Fort Wayne, Indiana. When this mission was well advanced, he set out northward to build a school and mission among the Potawatomies. The treaty for the mission land within the reservation, which then included parts of Niles and Buchanan, was signed by Chiefs Topinabee, Pokagon, and neighboring chiefs, along with government representatives. Rev. McCoy returned to Fort Wayne for his wife and children, several teachers, a few cattle, and a herd of pigs; and, at a salary of $600 a year began his work.

Very soon four houses, a school, and a blacksmith shop were built on the mission grounds; and before many months the mission had become not only a center for learning and religion, but a trading post as well.

Dedicated to the salvation and the preserved dignity of the Indian against the encroachment of the white man, Isaac McCoy fought a continuing and losing battle against the debilitating influence of the newcomers, especially the sale and trade of whiskey to his Indian friends. He and his teachers devoted themselves to teaching Christianity, improved agricultural methods, new usable crafts, better habits of industry and economy...in general trying to improve the lot of the hard-pressed natives.

It was inevitable that the mission, a lonely spot of civilization in a vast wilderness, should come to serve as a general supply center for explorers, and a stopping-off place for settlers seeking new land in the area. This crowding in of the new would-be settlers, and the continuous making of new treaties, with the Indians submitting to the demands of the white man, foretold the decline of the Indians' strength and their eventual removal to lands farther west. Further details of the last days of the Potawatomie nation in southwestern Michigan will be told in the next chapter.

At this point in our story we will only recount the historical record which tells us, without touching on the heartache behind the cold facts, that in 1836 Rev. McCoy was commissioned to lead a large group of the Potawatomies into Kansas; and that he remained there with his friends. In Kansas and Oklahoma Isaac McCoy established new Baptist missions among the Indians; and he and his son John, who later platted the original town of Kansas City, became well-known and eminent citizens of those territories.

Rev. McCoy, in his humanity and his courage, also left his mark upon the Niles-Buchanan area, in spite of his frustrating and heartbreaking endeavors at the Carey Mission on behalf of the Indians. Remembered by succeeding generations for his good works and his teachings, he also is remembered for the giving of his name to McCoy's Creek, which he visited in his rare free hours and "claimed" as his own private fishing grounds.

One of Isaac McCoy's most important contributions to the territory, history would indicate, was the establishment of the first grist mill in 190 miles.

By today's standards, this feat might seem insignificant; but consider, in retrospect, the problem of early settlers in grinding their grain into a useable form for cooking and baking. Most of Berrien County's early pioneers had come from the more urban East, and were unused to this particular hardship in preparing food. While they found here a good supply of meats, wild fruits, and vegetables, they keenly felt the want of baking materials, and at first resorted to the Indian method of pounding corn with stones; but this did not make very palatable Johnny cake.

Before 1825, there was no grist mill west of Ann Arbor. About 1824 at the Carey Mission, Rev. McCoy attempted to relieve the situation by shaping two large boulders so that one might be turned on the other by hand to grind corn.

The preacher himself said of this mill, "One strong man, by constant labor, was able to make corn meal of poor quality sufficient for one family". Wheat could not be ground at all.

The mission soon replaced this first "mill" by a more efficient one run by horsepower. With this mill, the first in Berrien County, more than 300 bushels of wheat were made into flour in 1825. This service was so much in demand that men from distant areas, with no roads to the Carey Mission, undertook to shoulder 100-pound bags of grain and carry them through the forests to Niles.

The beginnings of a new era in this territory can be measured from the building of the first real, water-powered grist mill on the Dowagiac Creek in 1827 by Eli Ford. Other eager and industrious pioneers were already studying the maps and tramping the countryside in search of the only power source then known...water; and very soon speculative eyes were turned toward the strong, pliant riffles of McCoy's Creek.

Chapter Three

THE GREAT LAND GRAB

If the Rev. Isaac McCoy in his building of the Carey Mission did indeed "open a gap in the wilderness", as has been written of him, then the settlers who followed close behind all but tore it asunder.

As the pioneers moved into the rich, fertile valley of the St. Joseph River...first as lone explorers, and then as whole families staking their claims upon the best lands...the newcomers began to look longingly at the remaining lands held in reservation for the Indians; and the government felt obliged to favor its westward-moving tide of citizens.

A treaty was signed in 1821 at Chicago by General Cass, Chiefs Topinabee and Weesaw, and 53 other chiefs, by which the Indians ceded to the United States all of the present Van Buren County and all of Berrien County lying east and north of the St. Joseph River, with some exceptions. The treaty also gave the government nine other counties and parts of five more, all in southwestern Michigan, as well as a strip ten miles south of the Michigan-Indiana line. The pay to the Indians for all this land amounted to about five cents an acre.

By a treaty made in 1828 at the Carey Mission, the Indians gave up all the remaining land except that lying between the river and a direct line running from the state line in the southwest corner of Bertrand Township northeast to the river in Section 12 of Buchanan Township. This tract contained nearly 50 sections, and included all but four sections of the Township of Bertrand and several sections in Buchanan and Niles townships.

Unfortunately for the Indians, this remaining reservation was considered by most settlers to contain the choicest land in southern Michigan.

In 1833, the Potawatomies were again called to Chicago, where they were persuaded to sign over the last of the reservation, whose lands included the future Buchanan. The most well-known chief of the Buchanan area, Chief Moccasin, was among those signing this last treaty which gave the Indians, in exchange, new lands in Kansas and Oklahoma. The treaty stipulated that the Potawatomies must move to the new lands within three years.

As noted in the last chapter, Rev. Isaac McCoy led the first of the Potawatomies into Kansas in 1836...in what some historians have referred to as "a death march". For a number of years thereafter the exodus westward continued; and by 1843, all except Chief Pokagon's band...and a few others who had received special concessions and land grants...had left their Michigan home for new reservations beyond the Mississippi.

In the intervening years, between the signing of the last treaty and the departure of the last Indians, a government land office had been established in Kalamazoo for the distribution of Indian lands; and there followed the great land boom of the 1830's, in which choice tracts were sold at $1.25 an acre. This land grab was later described by one writer as "a bonanza richer by far than all the gold fields of California".

Since the most valuable land of all was that containing controllable water...the only power source then known...many early settlers were eager to seize this source of livelihood to grind grain and saw wood. McCoy's Creek, a narrow stream with a rapid fall toward the river, looked just right for such purpose.

Buchanan's First Settler

The first settler in Buchanan Township, according to area histories, was Charles Cowles, who came to Niles from Vermont in 1832 and located at Buchanan in 1833, the same year the Indian reservation was abolished. He erected a cabin, and soon after a shingle mill, about a quarter-mile upstream on McCoy's Creek. (The site of this first mill is believed to have been located on land owned in later years by Mrs. Bert Spafford, who gave the land to the City of Buchanan several years ago to be used as a park. To date, the park has not been developed.)

Meantime, Russell McCoy (no relation to Rev. Isaac McCoy) had come from Virginia to Pokagon Prairie in 1829, and in 1830 to the Carey Mission, where he worked for some time as a general caretaker. He then engaged in boating on the river, and in 1833 located a "squatter's claim" and cleared a small tract of land at the mouth of McCoy's Creek. He built a cabin, and in 1834 began to build a sawmill in partnership with Hiram Wray, who had recently arrived with his wife and child.

The Cowles mill was in running order before that of McCoy and Wray, however; and the Cowles mill therefore became the settlement's first crude factory.

In the same year of 1834, John Hatfield and a Mr. Atkins located a claim near Cowles, and also built a sawmill.

Thus within a year or so, three mills had been built on McCoy's Creek; but none yet answered the most basic need of the settlers...the grinding of grain for food.

Cowles and Hatfield, after operating their mills for a short time, sold their properties to Dr. Charles Wallin.

Dr. Wallin, who came here with his family from New York state converted the Cowles mill into a grist mill and thus at last furnished the seedling community with corn meal and graham flour. The flour was bolted by hand. In addition to providing the first grist mill in the Buchanan area, Dr. Wallin became the settlement's first physician; and he served as the township's first supervisor when the latter was organized in 1837. He also built the first grist mill in Bertrand Township.

Others of the settlers who settled here in the first few years after the Treaty of Chicago were Seth Sherwood, who came in 1834 and located a mile north of Moccasin Bluff; John Hamilton, a millwright by trade, who came from Virginia in 1837; and Andrew Day, who came to Buchanan from Connecticut in 1836. Day worked at the McCoy mill at the mouth of the creek for some time; and in 1839 he and Hamilton erected a grist mill with "two runs of stone" at about the present site of the Clark Credit Corporation parking lot, which borders Days Avenue. (Of course there was no mill race dividing the creek at that time...nor a Days Avenue, nor any streets at all.)

Government Claims Land

All was not clear sailing...or rather we should say clear title...for our earliest residents, however. Much of the property in the first years was held under preemption rights, or "squatter's claims" which had been surveyed and occupied before the official land survey by the government; and Dr. Wallin and his neighbors discovered before 1840 that the government claimed their land.

The national government had appointed special commissioners to select certain valuable lands in the former Indian reservation to be granted to the new state of Michigan for the support of a new university later established at Ann Arbor. Without regard for the claims of settlers, the price of this land, which included the Wallin property, was raised to $12 and $15 an acre, under the jurisdiction of the University of Michigan.

A great clamour was raised at the injustice of depriving the settlers of hard-won properties, which in the Wallin case included the clearing, home, water power, and the mills on McCoy's Creek. Dr. Wallin and others spent all of one winter in Detroit, then the capital of the state, and finally succeeded in getting a relief bill passed by the legislature; but it was vetoed by Gov. Stephen T. Mason.

In choosing the best lands for the university, thus negating former agreements, the government and its surveyors had determined that the power of the St. Joseph River from Niles to the bend of the river north of Buchanan totaled 196 stone; and the power of McCoy's Creek was estimated at 24 stone, or one-eighth the power of the mighty river. (A "stone" is measured as the water power required to turn the upper stone or "runner" for a grain-grinding mill). The reason for the high power comparison between the river and the relatively small creek, as reported by the surveyors, was the fifty-foot fall along the length of the creek from the site of the present Co-ops mill to the mouth of the creek.

Dr. Wallin, who had contributed so much to the community as doctor, miller, and local government organizer, lost his property on the creek and in 1840 moved to Berrien Springs, the county seat. Here he began anew to make a home in Michigan, practicing his profession as a doctor in that village.

In the next chapter, we shall pause in our story to take a closer look at the Wallin family and those earliest years on McCoy's Creek.

As for Russell McCoy...he soon moved to Missouri, but returned in 1839. He engaged in farming for some years, then kept a store for a while in Buchanan, as well as a hotel. About 1856 he and several others bought 200 acres on the banks of Clear Lake three miles west of Buchanan and there built a steam sawmill. He died in Buchanan in 1873.

Many persons over the years have believed that the creek which courses through Buchanan was named for Russell McCoy, but this assumption is disproved in early maps of the area which designate the stream as McCoy's Creek after the arrival of the Rev. Isaac McCoy but before the appearance in these lands of Russell McCoy.

Chapter Four

THE WALLIN FAMILY OF McCOY'S CREEK

"The Indians would ride up to our cabin near the creek and beg mother for bread. If a loaf was forthcoming, they would race their ponies, throwing the bread high in the air ahead of them and catch it as it fell. Sometimes they came around drunk, insolent, and ugly, demanding with threatening gestures 'godamshug'. There was a loaf of sugar in the home, kept for unusual occasions of entertainment, and this was greatly coveted by the redskins.

"At times they would peer in at the windows and door of the schoolhouse, which was a mile away near the Indian village, and frighten the children. The teacher, Sarah Willet, who later became my stepmother, was not to be intimidated, however; and, armed with a stout whip cut in the woods, would drive away a whole group. It was not until 1840 that these last remnants of the tribe were removed to the western reservations."

The above recollections, taken from the book, "The Michigan Wallins" by Van A. Wallin, provide part of the only available description of the life of the earliest settlers in the Buchanan area between the years 1835 and 1840; and the quoted words were spoken by the author's father, Frank Wallin. Diaries and journals were not kept by the majority of task-burdened pioneers; and historians of later years, finding such incidents of day-to-day existance beyond the memories of the descendents, were forced to content themselves with only the facts and dates which were public record.

"The Michigan Wallins", a copy of which can be found in the Buchanan Public Library, was written by the grandson of Dr. C.C. Wallin, who came with his family in 1835 and bought the cabin and sawmill of the first Buchanan settler, Charles Cowles. The mill was converted by Dr. Wallin into a grist mill -- "small, but large enough to serve the needs of neighboring families".

The Wallin family, part of the tide of immigration streaming in from the East, left their home in Gilbertsville, New York, and traveled through the Erie Canal to Buffalo; thence by schooner to Detroit, and finally by team and wagon to the low hills and broad valleys of the St. Joseph, beginning their new life in the one-room log cabin near the creek. There were then no frame houses in the township. The cabin was located a quarter-mile upstream from where the creek empties into the river. A half-mile through the woods was the Potawatomie village of Chief Squaga, and a half-mile farther downstream on the river was the village of Chief Moccasin, below Moccasin Bluff, according to the Wallin book.

Wrote biographer Wallin of his grandfather's first Michigan home, "The one-room log house must have seemed poor indeed compared with the commodious, well-built home they had lived in in Gilbertsville. There was an attic overhead, reached by a permanent ladder on the wall. The boys Thomas, Frank, and Alfred slept there, with the parents and daughter Libby in the living room below."

Township Organized

It was in this tiny, rude log cabin, built four years earlier by Mr. Cowles, that a meeting was held April 3, 1837, for the purpose of organizing the township, since there were by then 27 white families homesteaded in the area. Dr. Wallin was the host and moderator; and Darius Jennings served as clerk. Fifteen votes were cast; and Dr. Wallin was named first supervisor of the township. Other elected officers included Jennings, S.S. Sherwood, John Hatfield, Charles Cowles, Absolem Colvin, William Wagner, and A.C. Day as constable.

In a letter written to his old home in New York early in 1838, Dr. Wallin declared, "I am much pleased with the country I live in. I don't know but it's the best county of land I know of in the United States, and I have seen a great many of them (but not all)."

He referred to Berrien County as great wheat country, not as cold as New York, and very healthy; and, he continued, "Wheat sells at $1.00; corn, not shelled, at four shillings, and oats at 3 6...and a ready cash market for all we have to sell at the door" (the grist mill).

The young doctor, who was also farmer, miller, politician, and lumberman, wrote, "Farmers make double the money here that they do in New York".

Later that year, however, the letters home told a different story, the Wallin book reveals.

We quote: "The 'sickly summer' of 1838, with the whole family in bed with the ague a large part of the time, had taken the hopeful note from messages back home. 'Fever and ague', or 'chills and fever'...the malaria of today...raged in the McCoy and nearby settlements, visiting almost every home and bringing death to many in the log cabins of the pioneers. All the Wallin family was afflicted. The epidemic became serious in May and continued on into the following January. The doctor himself was too sick to care for his practice much of the time, being too weak to ride; and further, was hampered by his inability to get medicine. Although quinine had been introduced into America only a few years earlier, still the doctor relied on the remedy and complained because he couldn't get it in sufficient quantities."

His son Thomas had written that year. "Mosquitoes very bad, and we fought them with a smudge. All the water came from the spring some rods away and down a steep hill, and we were often too weak to fetch it. No fruit except wild berries and dried apples. That summer took all the courage out of us."

And in a letter written early in 1839 Dr. Wallin declared, "Ague and fever of a very malignant character prevails in these rich countries. This year has taken many to their long home...I mean to try this country one more year, and if we continue to be sickly I shall then seek for some more healthy one."

The Wallin family did survive, and remained in the McCoy settlement for some time after, contributing needed courage and zeal to the growing community. Only when their lands, to which they had believed they held clear title, were claimed and revalued by the government were they forced to move to a new community. This was obviously a great loss to the McCoy's Creek settlement.

The Wallin family story, as told by letters and word of mouth and compiled into book form by one descendent, opened one small window into the obscure past to illuminate in vignette the many hardships and frequent heartbreak endured by the early settlers in the Buchanan area.

Chapter Five

"COY'S CREEK" BECOMES BUCHANAN

As the swiftly moving western line of civilization known as the American Frontier swept through the St. Joseph Valley, Buchanan lagged somewhat behind the building of Niles and other communities because this area, as part of the Potawatomie reservation, was not completely surveyed and cleared for settlement until the late 1830's. Also, many Indians still lingered near the settlement, causing some harrassment and fear, in their last vain attempt to hold their homeland.

But still they came...strong men of vision and industry whose names are heard yet today in the community...Leonard Madron, Daniel Roe, Lawson Watson, John and Robert Martindale, Jacob C. Dragoo, William Wagner, John Juday, Levi Sanford, Frederick Howe, A. Colvin, Darius Jennings, Russell Babcock, and others.

By 1840, the population of the township had reached 264; and five years later there were 630 persons in and around the McCoy's Creek settlement...or " 'Coy's Crick"...as the colony was called in the hurry-up jargon of the day. (However it was enunciated, the village continued to be identified for many years by the stream which gave it birth, at least until the coming of the railroads in 1849.)

Pioneer families poured in from the south, traveling the Fort Wayne Trail and the Chicago Trail to the Portage Prairie district, where they found fertile, level land and "burr oak openings" ready for planting without land-clearing to contend with. By 1834 the entire stretch of prairie land south of Buchanan was producing grain crops.

And they came from the east, our pioneers, many of English and New England stock, seeking the milling and craftsmen's trades in this new land. It was because of these mills that McCoy's Creek took on real stature and came into its own some 140 years ago.

It is difficult to imagine that the opening of the Erie Canal in 1825 would have an eventual, direct bearing on the eminence of little McCoy's Creek; but as it turned out the two streams, nearly a thousand miles apart, were joined not only by the flow of the tides, but also by the tide of immigration from the East...simply because of the accessibility of this area via the water route after the canal was completed.

Easterners who might have been content to remain behind were easily tempted to "go west" by the cheaper, safer, and usually more comfortable water route through the Great Lakes instead of the overland trails. Some travelers disembarked at Detroit and continued by stage and wagon, while others continued on through the Straits into Lake Michigan and came to the Buchanan area by keelboat up the St. Joseph River.

Village Platted

By 1842, there were a dozen buildings within the little village itself; and it was in that year that the plat for Buchanan was drawn up and recorded by the industrious and conscientious landholder and businessman, John Hamilton. Hamilton, as explained in an earlier chapter, was one of the settlement's first citizens...a millwright by trade who had come here from Connecticut in **1837 and** built a grist mill in partnership with Andrew Day.

The original town, according to available records, encompassed only the land bordered by Front Street on the south, Third Street on the north, Oak Street to the west, and the foot of Days Avenue on the east, a total of some 40 acres (the streets at that time had different names, also.) Large farms of a number of prominent citizens bordered the village limits; and some of these were annexed to the town within the next decade.

Hiram Weese, who arrived in 1837, built a log house near the river bluff in which school was taught in 1841 and 1842 by Angelina Bird, a popular school teacher in the early days. The first dry goods store in the village was opened in 1842 by the firm of Stanley, Staple, and Twombly. A hotel, the American House, was added to the village in 1844 by Garrett Morris; and before that...as early as 1840, a whiskey distillery was set up along McCoy's Creek, apparently very near the Hamilton-Day mill on what would one day become Days Avenue.

One droll writer of the local-scene-in-history once commented, "There was a well-worn path angling back to the distillery, and on the wall of the distillery hung a tin cup, which the casual guest was welcome to fill from the spigot. The distillery sat back on McCoy's Creek, to whose justly famous waters it was necessary to add only a little coloring to make first-class whiskey."

(In this more conservative narrative, however, we would hesitate to offer such lavish claims for the waters of The Real McCoy!)

As the village began to grow and take on stature in the 1840's, the creak of mill wheel and the roar of released water in the tail race could be heard up and down "the old mill stream". Flour dust and the dust of sawed lumber from the old "gash" and "muley" saws sifted over all...but not the dust of stagnation.

Along the waterway, which would continue to dominate the settlement for many years, dams and water wheels were eventually squeezed into almost every available rod of its last powerful mile. Since the water could be used over and over again, the power of the McCoy...and therefore the flouring and lumbering economy of the area, depended upon how many successive dams could be built, and the power developed at each.

Out in the countryside, lumbermen were beginning to harvest the heavy stands of timber for local and for Chicago markets. The lumber tagged for the city trade was rafted down the St. Joseph River and loaded on boats at St. Joseph for the trip across the big lake.

Locally, the growing prosperity enabled family after family to have planks sawed and shingles made in the local shingle mills so that they were able, within a few years after their arrival, to move the family from the old log house into the "big house".

In town, businesses sprang up almost overnight...and changed hands almost as often. Most of the new small enterprises were half-store-half-factory; and the merchant, with or without helpers, made the goods he or she sold.

Typical of this small-shop era in Buchanan were the establishments of the harness-makers, shoe-makers, tailors, dressmakers, milliners, watch-makers, barrel makers (or coopers, as they are called), blacksmith shops, and others.

Later, in the 1850's, there was even a hoop-skirt shop (when hoop-skirts were all the rage) run by Mrs. Philander P. Dunning, who manufactured her own product, and who later branched into the millinery business, continuing as a tradeswoman here for many years. (Today there are some in Buchanan who still remember with affection a later milliner, Mrs. Esther Parkinson, who went into business here in 1890 and continued until 1926, when she died...it is said...literally "with a thimble on her finger.")

During these mid-century years, the village grew in dimension also. Joseph DeMont's addition in 1849 extended the town limits to Portage Street (now Red Bud Trail North) on the east, to Fourth Street on the north, and to the old cemetery (now Kathryn Park) on the west. There was no street running south, other than Portage, as late as 1854. Day's addition, reaching from Front Street to the railroad, was added in 1856.

John Ross, who came to the town in 1845, built the first brick building, a store, in which he also kept the post office when he was named first postmaster in 1848.

During these years of embryonic growth, surveyors and officials had been laying plans, and tracks, for the Michigan Central Railroad across lower Michigan (as its name would indicate, the railroad had originally been slated to cross the state farther north). The route was completed south of the village and westward to New Buffalo in 1849.

At least one local historical source indicates that as the coming of the railroad approached reality, it became imperative to railroad officials and townsfolk alike that the settlement must have a station name of some stature; and that the rail men chose (with some political persuasion) the name of Buchanan in honor of James Buchanan, a politically active Democrat and statesman who had earned great respect for his work in securing statehood for the territory of Michigan (in 1837). On the other hand, it is reported that the town was named Buchanan fifteen years before the noted politician and ambassador became President of the United States in 1857. The original village was platted in 1842, so there is some question just how much the railroad had to do with the naming of the town. Either way, the village was still known as "McCoy's Creek" until dignified by the name of "Buchanan" appearing in large letters upon the rail depot building.

In the unsettled, "feast and famine" years before the Civil War, the town gained in substance. The start of the wagon-making factory of Jacob Luther in the early 1840's had already signaled the beginning of the heyday of wagon-makers in Buchanan; and the era of furniture making was just getting underway with the establishment of the Black and Willard Furniture Factory in 1860.

Churches were built, official schools established, and in spite of the advent of the Civil War, all was going swimmingly along "Old McCoy's Creek"...until the town was all but destroyed in "the big fire" of 1862.

Chapter Six

THE FLAMES OF FORTUNE... OF WAR... AND OF TIMBERS

Toward the middle of the 19th century, the spirited sloshing of mill wheels along McCoy's Creek had become the heart valves of the town, pumping life into one growing, not-yet-adolescent child of the "new West", known as Buchanan. But even then, before 1850, the "youngster" community was reaching out to, and taking nourishment from, the world which surrounded it.

The Chicago Trail south of town and other nearby stagecoach lines brought a constant stream of visitors and investors into the town, while just to the north and east, the booming river traffic on the St. Joseph was providing an increasing flow of goods and new settlers to the entire area. Keelboats, paddle wheelers, and log rafts plied the fast, deep waters between distant upriver towns and St. Joseph at the river mouth, connecting there with schooners of the Great Lakes. From the south of town came the prosperous farmers of the Portage Prairie to do business with the grain and lumber mills and small shops in the town. To the west and northwest stretched great, rich forests of whitewood, walnut, hard maple, and oak...and the harvesting and exploitation of the woodlands was just beginning.

Another, unforeseen and propitious event for the village was the coming of the railroad, as discussed in the last chapter, which brought to within walking distance the only railroad in southwestern Michigan.

In the village itself, horse and oxen teams pulled loaded wagons through the few rutted streets and across the crude plank bridges over McCoy's Creek. The creek itself then followed a meandering path from the southwest, angling eastward and bordering a swampy area between Days Avenue and Portage Street behind the present Record office...part of the farm pasture of Andrew Day, whose home was located on the corner at the present site of the Gamble store.

This was a village of farms, with almost as many barns as houses. Cows and pigs earned their keep on street glades or in the woods, strengthening the families' resources. A three-block cluster of mill workers' houses north of McCoy's Creek formed the village plat until mid-century.

Earlier, the school children had been removed from the former log blacksmith shop of Hiram Weese north of town near the river to a new frame schoolhouse within the town (generally believed to have been located at 305 Main Street). This latter school served the town until the completion of the Union School (later known as the Dewey School) in 1856.

A new, larger cemetery, Oak Ridge, had been acquired and surveyed by Edward Ballengee to replace the former burial grounds at the present Kathryn Park; and the post office located in the mercantile establishment of John D. Ross was reporting increased business over the $12 reported in its first year.

In 1845, the population of Buchanan had been 630; and nine years later, in 1854, it had more than doubled to 1,282, according to Cowles' "History and Directory of Berrien County", printed here in 1871.

Village Incorporated

When a new surge of growth hit Buchanan shortly before the beginning of the Civil War, the leaders of the community determined that a need for local government was at hand. The village was incorporated March 3, 1858; and the newly elected village officers, headed by President James M. Matthews, gave their attention to such matters as installing cinder or wooden sidewalks, real bridges across McCoy's Creek, some fire control methods, and the general peace and safety of the growing settlement. Action was taken on impounding cattle, chickens, and hogs running loose during certain hours through the town; and trees were grubbed from the middle of the newer streets.

The Mill Race

During the summer of 1857, when men around the blacksmith shop and the Hamilton-Day mill were chewing straws and talking politics...when words like "Black Republican" and "Abolitionist" and "Copperhead" were starting to be heard...when the town had an uncertain air even as the children of the village happily waded in the marsh behind the Day homestead and unconcernedly sucked on the sweet flag roots they dug there...through such a summer, a ship was bound from England carrying William Bainton from his home at Walton Abbey, Yorkshire.

Bainton, a miller by trade, was migrating to Michigan for the purpose of starting a flour mill in the new land. Upon arriving in Buchanan, the young man immediately set about obtaining water rights on McCoy's Creek. With the help of a Mr. Beach, hired workers, and teams of horses and oxen, Bainton excavated the mill race, thus dividing the creek in the western part of town, and built the headgates down behind the site of the present high school to control the flow through each branch.

By 1858, the mill race and the mill (the present Co-ops mill) were near completion. Bainton, according to his grandson Kelsey Bainton, had made several trips back to England before settling in Buchanan, bringing on his final crossing "a roll of stone". These mill stones from the quarries of England, five feet in diameter and two-and-a-half feet thick, were brought through the St. Lawrence, around through the Great Lakes and down Lake Michigan, and up the St. Joseph River to their new home on McCoy's Creek.

Although very little of the original mill and falls remains today, the first Bainton mill (later the Pears mill) is the only one to survive to the present, all others having been destroyed by fire during the past hundred years.

William Bainton operated the mill until his death in 1865; and in 1868 it was taken over by a family friend and fellow Britisher, William Pears. He in turn was succeeded by the firm of Pears and Rough.

At first the mill was powered by a big "breast" wheel, 14 feet wide, over which the water dropped 16 feet. The mill was known in the early years as The Rural Milling Company, and the product bore the brand name of "Diadem Flour". For years the entire output of this mill was shipped to England, homeland of both millers, Bainton and Pears. The mill had a maximum daily production capacity of 100 barrels of flour weighing 196 pounds each, the manufacture of which required an intake of 500 bushels of wheat daily. Barrels for the flour were made in the local cooper shops operated by Joe Voorhees, Jay Glover, and Nicholas Arney.

At that time there was an alley running south from Front Street to the mill, just opposite the intersection of Main and Front. The building which formerly housed the Hollywood Theatre now stands on the former alley entrance. A bridge was built across the rail race below the wheel for farmers to drive through the alley and across the bridge with their loads of wheat.

After the death of William Bainton, his young sons William F. and Charles L. Bainton determined to carry on the traditional family trade, and in later years built the large Bainton mill farther downstream, which continued in business until 1924. This mill will be discussed in a later chapter.

War and The Great Fire

Dark and troubled days came to Buchanan in the early 1860's. Rumors, impromptu street-corner speeches, torchlight parades, angry newspaper editorials from the East, and harsh words, pitting neighbor against neighbor, preceded the enlisting of many local sons and brothers to serve in the Civil War.

Adversity never seems to travel on a lone ill wind...and so it was in Buchanan.

In 1860, a cabinet shop had been built on the south side of the tail race of the original Bainton mill. The shop was run by an overshot water wheel, getting water from the head flume of the flour mill. In late October, 1862, stray sparks ignited the sawdust in the cabinet shop. The flames spread rapidly, missing the flour mill but igniting and destroying all the buildings on Front Street from Main to Days on the south, Main to the creek on the north, and on up to Dewey Avenue...about 20 buildings in all, including the new three-story brick storebuilding of Ross, Clark, and Alexander on the northeast corner of Main and Front Streets. The strong wind carried sparks as far as the other side of the river, where a barn was burned to the ground. Men, women, and children turned out to save what could be saved. It was reported that one daring young lady led the horses from the livery stable of Julius Russell up the Niles Road and tied them to trees.

When it was over, nearly all the business section of the village lay in smoke and ashes.

With a stubborn persistence typical of their New England heritage, many of the tradesmen began to build again, bigger and finer shops than before. Even before the end of the war, much of the village stood proudly arrayed in new brick and mortar, with richly corniced store fronts, along with several fine brick residences throughout the town.

In the years ahead, the course of the creek would continue to be altered, and nudged this way and that to accommodate new enterprises...but there would continue to be space...and time...for small boys to sneak down to "the 'ol swimmin' hole", to hook "granddaddy" trout and "ride the flume"...for young girls to gather watercress and berries along the banks for nibbling...for men and women to join the young people in gay skating parties on frozen ponds diverted from the mainstream...for pleasures to almost offset the hardships of the pioneer settlement's first three decades...and those yet to come.

And little McCoy's Creek, having started it all, gurgled happily along unaware that it was soon to meet its match with the coming of steam power.

Chapter Seven

POST-WAR BOOM ALONG "THE OLD MILL STREAM"

By the time the torn and tormented years of the Civil War were ended in 1865, Buchanan was ready...both in substance and in spirit...to enjoy the Good Life. It came, with all its manifestations; and the town "boomed".

Buchanan was described in those post-war years variously as: "the best business town in southern Michigan", "the second largest furniture center in Michigan" (next to Grand Rapids), "the horse-race and gambling center of the mid-west", "the wickedest town in the state", "the town with more churches than saloons", "the printing center of the middle west", and a few more superlatives... and invectives.

Little McCoy's Creek, which started it all, was described in the 1871 publication "Berrien County History and Directory" by Edward Cowles, as being "one of the most improved water powers in the state".

Buchanan, typical of the towns of that hand-labor and one-owner shop era, was a town of contradictions. There were the very rich, and the very poor; and the "middle class", so hugely dominant today, was then almost nonexistant. There was much hardship and deprivation to be found on the poorer farms around the town; and in the village, many millworkers and factory hands endured low wages and frequent layoffs. Nevertheless, the overall picture in post-war Buchanan was one of prosperity and enjoyment.

A leisure class had grown up within the town by 1870, thanks to the progress of the lumber and flour mills and the early success of the wagon and furniture-making factories, even though the women of the community's poorer families were still making tallow candles, soap, and handwoven clothing, with their men spending back-breaking hours grubbing stumps from their land, and harvesting the fields by hand.

In the late 60's and 70's, the community had apparently emerged from the raw pioneer era, but the attentive ear could still hear the echo of the trailblazer's axe.

The Forest Bonanza

Within a few short years after the end of the Civil War, Buchanan was taking full advantage of the surrounding forests, which were recognized as possessing the best hardwood timber in Michigan, and possibly in the United States. The businesses in the village and the people who owned the land were mining out a bonanza in the finest lumber, and finding easy markets with convenient transport via the nearby railroad and the St. Joseph River. The farmers of the timberlands eagerly cleared their lands of splendid timber, cut it into logs, and hauled it to town during the winter to the furniture factories. These factories therefore paid out practically all money for materials to local people; and this in turn stimulated other local businesses. Thus, while the farmers were depleting the land of woodlands that had taken centuries to grow, the community rode through the depressions of the 70's, 80's, and early 90's without serious notice.

The Whistles of Old McCoy

A local woman once wrote to the Record that when her father came to Buchanan in the late 1860's, steam whistles representing as many various industrial enterprises blew every morning. The majority were sawmills and grist mills, with a sprinkling of sash and blind factories and wagon works. He had recalled that in those days the whistle was the main part of the factory. Every one saw to it that it had a good whistle, which was blown frequently, even though it might be necessary to stop the machinery to blow it.

For many years, as has been stated earlier, the first factories were built along McCoy's Creek, which was a somewhat larger stream a century ago than it is today due, perhaps, to the heavy forests of that time which held back and channeled the snow and rainfall. With the advent of steam power in the late 60's, however, local manufacture was soon no longer dependent upon the power generated by the creek.

An "Atlas of Berrien County," published in 1873 by C.O. Titus, contains a map of the village of Buchanan, with McCoy's Creek as the main artery of its being...a creek divided, concentrated, dammed up, spread out, moved this way and that...to accommodate a dozen enterprises along its length.

A wool-carding mill was located at Bakertown, near the headwaters; and the creek ran a free and meandering course eastward from there until it reached the headgates and the beginning of the mill race in the valley behind the present Buchanan High School. From there the stream followed a divided course to the center of town.

The map of 1873 shows a planing mill on the west side of Oak Street between Smith and Alexander streets, a saw and planing mill on the east side of Oak between Alexander and Chicago streets, a sash and blind factory on the west side of Oak between Chicago and Alexander streets on the mill race, and the Pears and Rough grist mill (present site of Co-ops mill).

After passing under Front Street at Days Avenue, the reunited stream formed a mill pond and dam behind the present Art's Rexall store, and was divided again as it crossed Portage (now known as Red Bud Trail North). The Fulton and Kingery grist mill (making Indian Reserve Flour) was then located on the east side of Portage, near the present entrance to Clark Equipment Company.

The creek then flowed as a single stream a short distance to a large mill pond on the Bainton estate (behind the present Wilt's grocery on today's Clark land). At the far eastern end of the pond was a dam serving the H.S. Black Factory (manufacturers of bedsteads, lounges, extension tables, stands, desks, etc.) Another grist mill was indicated farther downstream, with a sawmill at the mouth of McCoy's Creek where it enters the river.

Included on the map of a near-century ago was a half-mile horse-race track south of the large mill pond, a cheese factory on North Portage, and three hotels...the Tremont House (site of Sexton's Furniture), the Cottage Hotel on Main, and the Dunbar House (where the Clark Equipment Credit Corporation now stands).

A business directory, printed beneath the map of Buchanan, included:

Buchanan Manufacturing Company; J. Brown, (manufacturer of upholstery goods, dealer in looking glasses, picture frames, and baby carriages).

LEOPOLD POKAGON, 1775-1841,
CHIEF OF THE POTTAWATOMIE INDIANS
NORTHERN INDIANA HISTORICAL SOCIETY,
SOUTH BEND, INDIANA

LANDMARK OF OLD . . . A horse-watering trough for travelers, from a spring at the base of Moccasin Bluff. This was the site of Chief Moccasin's Indian village.

THE DEWEY SCHOOL . . . Buchanan's first Union School, pictured in 1945.

BUCHANAN's first high school . . . On Chicago Street. An architectural drawing, 1871.

PAVING DAYS AVENUE . . . The steam-powered tractor machine was owned and operated by Ben Tumbleson.

GOAT POWER . . . Clayton McCollum, Mark Treat, and Jack Purks enjoyed one-way rides only, as the goat would only pull the sleigh back home to the McCollum Livery Stable, and had to be led to some distant point to the boys could get a ride.

THE OLD RIVER STREET BRIDGE . . . At the turn of the century. The bronze plaque at the top reads: "1894, John McFallon, Highway Com'r; George B. Richards, Supervisor; Harry Binns, Clerk." The larger sign says, "$25 Fine For Driving On This Bridge Faster Than A Walk."

ZINC COLLAR PAD MANUFACTORY . . . The sign above the entrance announces one of the town's most enduring industries. Established in 1870, the factory was for almost a half-century located at the southwest corner of Oak and Chicago streets. Today the renovated building houses several rental apartments.

BLACK MANUFACTURING COMPANY . . . In the 1870's and 80's, thrived as a volume manufacturer of furniture. Pictured at its first location on the north side of the mill pond, off of River Street, this company, which was later changed to the Black and Willard Furniture company, was moved to Front Street, occupying the former Floral Hall and Rink buildings.

CELFOR TOOL COMPANY . . . And how it grew, on its way to becoming the giant Clark Equipment Company.

FIRST ELECTRIC POWER HOUSE . . . On the east bank of the St. Joseph River, Buchanan.

THE BUCHANAN BLUES . . . The baseball scourge of Michiana, put Buchanan "on the map" in the early years of this century.

THE BUCHANAN CONCERT BAND . . . A social institution around 1920. Those identified include: Fred Mead, Pete Fuller, and Leland Cassler, front row; also John Morris, Phay Graffort, Louis Runner, Ward Conrad, and Martin Lenz.

LIMOUSINE SERVICE IN THE GOOD OLD DAYS . . . Known as "Bird's Bus", this horse-drawn coach regularly met all trains and carried passengers from the station to the hotel, around the turn of the century. This hotel, located at the corner of Days and Front streets (at the present site of the Clark Credit Corporation) changed hands many times over the years of its existence. At the time of this photo, it was known as The Earl Hotel.

AN EARLY VIEW . . . Brodrick Drugs. The signs in front advertise "Drugs, Stationery, Toilet Articles, Ice Cream Soda, Cigars, Perfumery".

THE CLARK EQUIPMENT COMPANY BAND . . . Now just a melodious memory of "The Good Ol' Days."

UNVEILING OF THE TOWN CLOCK . . . Corner of Main and Front streets, August 23, 1913.

RAIL DISASTER... Death and injuries were the result when, in 1913, the Pere Marquette ("Pumpkin Vine") train traveling from St. Joseph to Buchanan encountered an open switch and was shunted onto the Clark Equipment spur line, slamming into a rail car as it as being loaded, near the Clark water tower.

INDIAN MAIDEN... Agnes Topash, who later became the matriarch of a well-known family in Buchanan, pictured in 1905, at age 16, at Magician Lake near Dowagiac.

TWO KINDS OF HORSEPOWER AT WORK . . . Construction of the present Buchanan power plant building on the east side of the St. Joseph River was started before the turn of the century and completed in 1902. In the center of this photo, construction of the wheel pits was underway, with the mill race area in the foreground. The old wooden dam, built in 1893, is at upper left and at the right, looking west across the river, is the Lee & Porter Axle Works, which burned in 1913. Power to the axle works was supplied by a long rope pulley running up the river bank. The original 10-foot dam and power plant were built by Buchanan Power and Electric Company, headed by John Holmes and Peter English. Charles A. Chapin purchased the facilities in 1902. In 1907 the old wooden dam was washed out by a flood and replaced with the present concrete structure. In that same year, according to company records, the company was merged with the present Indiana and Michigan Electric Company.

In 1905, the electric company had three employees and 75 customers.

MILL POND IN DRY SEASON . . . Photographed from the Pere Marquette railroad trestle, this view of the former mill pond on the present site of Clark Equipment Company includes the Bainton Niagara Mills in the background, looking east.

POWER PLANTS OLD AND NEW . . . Buchanan's first power plant on the St. Joseph River is pictured, center, with the newer facility under construction at the left, in 1902.

THE OLD ROUGH OPERA HOUSE . . . As it was just before the third floor, which housed the opera house, was removed from the building for safety's sake in the 1960's.

THE GIRLS BEHIND THE MEN BEHIND THE GUNS . . . Part of a Fourth of July parade during World War I.

THE NETTIE JUNE . . . A smaller excursion boat than the May Graham, with a large pontoon raft for passengers alongside. This photo is captioned, "Nettie June Steamer, built 1884 by Andy Carothers, used on the St. Joseph River."

MAY GRAHAM . . . A popular side-wheeler excursion boat on the St. Joseph River, ready to take on passengers near Batchelor's Island.

BUCHANAN's railroad station. In its heyday.

BUCHANAN'S POST OFFICE IN 1906.

VIEWS OF DOWNTOWN BUCHANAN . . . Photographed between 1900 and 1912.

Buchanan Wagon and Manufacturing Company (wagons, carriages, sleighs, repairs. D.E. Beardsley, proprietor).

Berrien County Record (Wagner and Kingery, publishers).

Richards and Fox (J.N. Valley's Patent Clothes Bars).

Zinc Collar Pad Factory ("Patented...warranted to cure the worse cases of sore neck". G.H. Richards, supt.)

Bent Wood Trunk Co. (manufacturer of Clark's patented bent wood trunks, burial caskets, sewing machine covers).

Morley and Talbot Foundry.

David Ebersol (manufacturer of T.P. Wilcox' Patent Water Elevator).

A washing machine and wringer factory was indicated on the map, on East Front Street, but was not listed in the directory. According to the directory, Buchanan in 1873 had eight physicians and surgeons. Groceries and dry goods were vended by the firms of H.J. Howe, Redden and Graham, Binns and Roe, S.L. Estes, and Smith and Sons. There were two livery barns; and the directory included a heavily printed advertisement for:

"J. Jones, proprietor of Barber Shop and Bath Rooms...Warm and cold baths at all times. Also in Connection, a first class Dye house. Ladies and Gents' garments colored and cleaned, and Dyed to order. Opposite the Dunbar House."

The "Ins" and "Outs" of Business

One thing is certain in researching a history of McCoy's Creek...and therefore of Buchanan itself...business ventures in early Buchanan involved an astoundingly intricate maze of "here-today-gone-tomorrow" schemes and enterprises, enough to boggle the minds of both the historical writer and the reader; and this writer will not attempt to catalogue each change of product, change of ownership, or change of locality during the ensuing decades.

A few stayed on...businesses which became an integral force in the building of Buchanan...or individuals who themselves became a part of the growing community through various ventures and by setting their roots in the community.

One such lasting industry was the Zinc Collar Pad Factory, which began production in 1870 and continued profitably and with wide renown until horses were no longer used as a prime source of work power and transportation 55 years later. Captain George Roberts opened his first shop near the railroad tracks on South Oak Street, and later moved his factory to the corner of Oak and Chicago streets, into the building which later became the "Virginia Apartments". Capt. Richards purchased the large brick home on Front Street built by Charles Clark, a pioneer merchant (this is now the Swem-Smith Funeral Home). The large Richards family became a popular and influencial segment of the saga of Buchanan, both socially and economically. The collar pad factory itself, by 1880, was producing 100,000 horse collar pads annually.

Berrien County Record

As Buchanan grew, advancing "from the water wheel to the dynamo in 120 years", only one business enterprise, begun in the town's early years, has survived to the present time.

The Berrien County Record, which celebrated its 100th year of publication under that name during 1967 was preceded, in its own lineage, by several owners who changed its name at will to suit the temper of the times.

The first publisher-editor in Buchanan was Alonzo Bennett, who moved his printing equipment here from New Buffalo in about 1857, setting up shop in the Tremont Hotel and calling his paper The Buchanan Vindicator.

This writer has also found some hazy historical reference to another paper begun that same year, the Buchanan Independent, established by J.M. Potter, also of New Buffalo; but this paper, if it in fact existed beyond a hopeful declaration of intention, was of short duration. During the Civil War, Bennett sold out to Lloyd and Turner, who appropriately changed the name of the Vindicator to Buchanan Weekly Union. D.A. Wagner took over in 1866, and in February, 1867, issued the first number of the Berrien County Record. A later publisher-editor, J.G. Holmes, changed the name only briefly in the late 1880's to Buchanan Record, but returned shortly to the name which marks the masthead today.

Competitive newspapers, such as The Buchanan Argus were in operation from time to time during the past century; and at one time there were three newspapers and job-printing plants in the town. In the 1870's, the village was the center of production of religious magazines for the middle west. The Advent Christian Church housed a printing plant producing "The Advent Times" and the "Advent Christian Quarterly".

In addition to the weekly newspaper, the Berrien County Record printed "The Christian Proclamation", a monthly journal for the Christian Church throughout the West.

HOMECOMING PARADE UNIT OF 1910 . . . **In their rush to join the parade through Buchanan, Kelsey and Charles Bainton appear to have left a letter out of the company's banner.**

Chapter Eight

ENTERTAINMENT A CENTURY AGO
(la gauche to la grande)

Buchanan was a lively town in the latter part of the last century, before the advent of "Dobbin's downfall...or "Ford's folly", which finally opened highways and throttles and a search for new horizons.

The people of the town and of the farming communities in the last century were dependent upon each other and upon their own invention for good times; and a study of local memoirs reveals that they never seemed to lack inspiration for fun and entertainment. Although the men worked 12 to 16 hours daily in the shops or fields...and "women's work was never done"...there were plenty of opportunities for hoedowns, frolics, cotillions, barn raisings, husking bees and the like. A Sunday walk to the river was a favorite Sabbath pastime for sweethearts or families; and even "going up to the station to meet the 5:15" provided adequate excitement.

One old-timer wrote in a letter to the Record, "In wintertime, which was the best time to get the logs out of the woods and into sawmills along McCoy's Creek, the heavy loads of logs would cut the roads up into 'thank-you-moms' and 'kiss-me-quicks', which made it very interesting for the younger set when they were out for a buggy ride with their best girls. I remember that most of the logs came from the north of town when I was a kid, and that was always the road I would take when going out with my girl, so that we might see how many of those 'kiss-me-quicks' we could find."

There was fun for the younger children, too, who were usually included in any church parties or get-togethers enjoyed by their elders, (as well as quite a few diversions of their own that would have turned the elders gray, had they known.)

Claude Roe once described some of these latter diversions of the boys in town, who were drawn to the wonders of McCoy's Creek, and an occasional huge sturgeon in the lower reaches to outsmart and to wrestle to shore; and there was the "ol' swimmin' hole" at the headgates back of the school, where the clean, clear water came rushing thru in mighty swirls. His letter of reminiscence appeared in the Record.

Mr. Roe recalled, "Many a good plank was purloined from the stacks of lumber back of the saw mill on South Oak Street along the creek, placed in the stream, and two or more young truants from school would mount the plank, shoes and stockings safely (?) resting on the plank beside them; and with long poles they would push their craft downstream, passing under the bridges on Oak and Chicago streets, one branch of which passed back of Dr. Roe's house on Oak where embankments had been made and the creek was several feet above the level of the ground on each side. This was exciting pleasure, going down through here. Soon we came to the old 'calaboose' and to the real thrill of the trip, getting the plank thru and past the Pears grist mill down in town. There was a headrace at this place, a regular flume made of planks, and the water ran pretty fast through here. Then we let the plank go its own way and we ran around the mill and caught up with it again down back of Noble's store, and once more were on our way. Then we passed back of the old hotel which was run at that time I think by Andy Carothers. Here where the two branches came together, we started the dark passage under Front Street at Days Avenue. Then we went down past the Slater home, past Kingery's mill and down through Bainton's mill pond, managing to get over the falls there and down the line, ever gaining speed on the way, passing another mill there just this side of Black's old home, and on down on our perilous trip; and there before us was the old St. Joe River itself. This was too much for our slippery craft and we pushed up to the banks and hopped off, giving the plank a final push, and away it went on its trip downstream at the mercy of the old St. Joe."

For the young girls, favorite memories were of a more genteel nature, like those of Esther Montague, member of a pioneer family, who recalled that the girls "were like a garden of bright flowers in hoops, pantalettes, and Shaker bonnets" for the first church supper held in Buchanan in 1860, on the lawn of the then new Methodist Church on Days Avenue.

The flourishing mills, factories, and shops in Buchanan in the latter part of the 1800's created a comfortable prosperity among those in the position of owner or manager, and a leisure class of social leaders quickly developed, with always a party to look forward to. A favorite diversion was the sleigh ride in winter, followed by an oyster supper. Excursions and picnics of all kinds were popular. Horse-drawn drays would be engaged for trips to Clear Lake; and there were many private as well as church or lodge-sponsored excursions down the river, or by rail to Diamond Lake.

In the summer croquet matches were held on the broad lawn next to the John D. Ross mansion (now City Hall). The Ross lawn extended to the corner of Front and Oak streets (the new city park square) and back to the mill race on the south. Here strawberry and ice cream festivals were held in the late 70's, as well as Saturday afternoon band concerts. The Ross property came to be known as the town square, providing a convenient "stage" for the Buchanan Concert Band. (Can it be a sign of "progress" that our modern square is designed to be merely ornamental?)

The Buchanan Cornet Band was organized in the late 60's, and all through the 70's and 80's was present to play for almost every official and social occasion, including river boating parties and birthdays...and to welcome distinguished visitors at the train station. The cornet band was apparently a social institution, its members playing only for the glory of belonging and a love of playing. Singing groups were also popular and in demand; and these included the Buchanan Serenaders and The Roe Family Singers.

Literature and Drama

On April 7, 1870, a Young Men's Literary Society was organized in Buchanan for the purpose of establishing an educational lecture course and providing a reading room to study the best periodicals of the day. This was strictly a masculine cultural endeavor; but before the second meeting, it became apparent that the young men of Buchanan had decided to enliven the proceedings by including the women, for in the Record report of the next meeting, several feminine committeemen were named. Literary clubs flourished, and they were for many years of mixed membership instead of for women only, as are today's literary groups. A Buchanan Dramatic Association was formed in the winter of 1876; and they soon presented as their first dramatic offering for the edification of the village the moralistic drama, "All That Glitters Is Not Gold".

Floral Hall and Rink

In compiling a history of McCoy's Creek, it is gratifying to report still another benefit to the town, thanks to the kind versatility of our subject. In the fall of 1869, a combination social hall and ice skating rink was built near the center of town by the Buchanan Park Association. The association was not a civic group, but gentlemen banded together to promote horse racing. They had built a half-mile track covering much of the site of the present Clark plant, known as the Bainton orchard. The Floral Hall and Rink was located just north of Front Street (near the Clark plant and approximately where the Clark greenhouse was later built. The greenhouse, too, is now just a memory.)

The Floral Hall was an eight-sided structure, 70 feet in diameter, almost of circular shape...two stories high, with the second story forming a gallery around the circumference. Surmounting the roof was a cupola observatory, and around the walls were 32 large windows. In the winter the hall was flooded by means of an Archimedes' screw, a device which lifted water from McCoy's Creek through a wooden cylinder fitted on the inside with a tight-fitting screw which turned by the use of a steam engine.

Said the Record of that year, "The Floral Hall and Skating Rink will exceed anything of the kind in western Michigan."

Enthusiasm continued, as the Record reported in 1870, "We doubt whether a finer skating park and more comfortable arrangement for skaters can be found anywhere in the state. It is expected to have a grand skating carnival soon. There is no place like the skating park for spending the afternoon in good, wholesome, and innocent enjoyment. Let the children skate, and the old folks, too. It won't hurt them and will do them good."

In the summertime, a fair was held on the grounds, and the Floral Hall and Rink was used for displaying horticultural and handiwork exhibits.

The old Floral Hall and Rink was later used as a furniture factory by the firm of Black and Willard when the factory moved from its former River Street address; and the hall was torn down about 1900 by Ed Willard.

The "Beehive"

In 1884, the roller skating craze struck Buchanan to the extent that the firm of Bishop and Fisk came here from Union City and erected a skating rink opposite the Spencer and Barnes factory on Days Avenue. The rink, 40 by 110 feet, was opened in December, 1884, and soon became known as "The Beehive". The rink was frequented by large crowds that year; but later the popularity of the sport waned and the rink was closed. "The Beehive" came back to life for a while in 1899 when it was taken over and re-opened by the Richardson Ball Bearing Skate Company.

Bicycles were just coming into use in the 1880's, causing a sensation comparable to the appearance of today's sleekest, newest sports cars. In 1881, when there were seven two-wheelers in Buchanan, Record Editor J.G. Holmes ran a scathing editorial on the traffic dangers caused by the reckless riding of bicycles on the sidewalks.

WINTER SPLENDOR . . . A modern view of McCoy's Creek meandering through Buchanan.

Chapter Nine

SOCIAL AND SOCIOLOGICAL TENOR OF A GROWING TOWN

Before the turn of the century in old Buchanan, a well-known joke among the townspeople used some of the most prominent citizens as its culprits. Often heard was, "Welcome to 'R' town"...or perhaps "You won't catch them napping in 'R' town!"...with a few variations on the pun.

The good-natured jibe was triggered by the fact that predominate among the social, business, and political leaders were the families of Ross, Roe, Redden, Rough, Richards, and Reynolds.

In the Rough family itself, there were David, William, Solomon, J.C. (Jake), and George...all enterprizing men who caused the clan name to become attached to almost every kind of local business in the 19th century, at one time or another. Most durable among the family ventures were the Rough Wagon Works and the Rough Opera House.

The Rough Opera House was unquestionably the center of public social life in Buchanan from the late 60's until the early 1900's. Located on the third floor of the brick building erected around 1860 by Perry Fox and Philander Weaver (the building now housing the Jo Dee's dress shop), the opera house was appointed with red plush seats, vaulted ceilings, and four ornamental iron pillars, with a stage at one end.

In its heyday, the walls of the celebrated theatre echoed to the voices of famous and near-famous speakers, including among the former Schuyler Colfax, who became national vice president under Grant. Perhaps no less thrilling was the appearance in the opera house of the one-and-only Tom Thumb, parading his minute form across the stage.

Churches sponsored fairs in the opera house to pay their pastors' salaries; and for many years graduation exercises and school musical and dramatic programs were held in the opera house. Here the voluminously bloomered stars of Buchanan's Girls' Basketball Team daintily battled girls of neighboring towns to bring glory to their own; and here also the politically fervent Greenbacks staged their campaigns in the 1870's.

To this theatre, in long succession, came the Irish comedies, Negro or burnt-cork minstrels, the Dutch dialect burlesques, the rube shows, the annually resurrected versions of "Uncle Tom's Cabin", and the solemn and sonorous lectures so dear to the hearts of our grandfathers.

In one of the most spectacular interpretations of "Uncle Tom's Cabin", Little Eva was lifted to heaven on a wire; and Eliza leapt across a cast-iron water tank (representing the ice-choked Ohio River) while real bloodhounds bayed at her heels, according to the Record's "drama critic" of the time.

In 1892 J.C. (Jake) Rough took over the opera house, making several improvements in the facilities. The following year, in 1893, Record Editor John Holmes' dream of electric lights for Buchanan had materialized with the building of the river dam; and electric lights were the wonder of the town.

That year, there was shown at the Rough Opera House in glorious, electrical, spectacular drama the opera "Faust", with mystically lighted effects to heighten the weirdness of the "vision of Marguerite" scene, and "the transformation of Faust".

During the 80's the opera house had been the scene of Buchanan's first demonstration of the Edison Talking Machine; and later, in the early years of this century, there was seen at the opera house the first motion pictures ever shown in Buchanan.

It was not long after that that the nickelodeons invaded the town...and the glory of Rough Opera House departed forever. In later days a dance floor was installed, and it became first a popular dancing place, and later a rowdy ballroom and skating rink. Eventually it was closed off altogether.

In 1964 the third floor of the building, the scene of unforgettable former glories, was removed from the building for safety's sake by a later owner.

The Narrow Gauge Railroad

Before passing by the social scene as it was in the late 19th century, it must be noted that the May 12, 1881, issue of the Record announced that the rails for the "Narrow Gouge" railway (a prophetic typographical error) had been laid from the Michigan Central northward across McCoy's Creek and as far as the old Potawatomie campgrounds, and that work by the St. Joseph Railway Company was proceeding at the rate of a quarter mile a day.

On May 14, the first excursion party rode a work train as far as Moccasin Bluff or Potawatomie Flat, as it was known. The next Sunday, The Good Templars boarded the train at River Street for a picnic on the river; and the following week, a crowd of 100 to 200 took the trip. On June 30, the women of the Presbyterian Church sponsored a "moonlight excursion" over the narrow gauge to the Eurastus Kelsey farm. The Buchanan Cornet Band went along to furnish music. The round trip cost 10 cents, and the ice cream and cake served by the ladies was 10 cents. The sponsors were jubilant, as 150 tickets were sold.

When the railway was completed to Berrien Springs, a series of very popular excursions to St. Joseph began. Passengers went by narrow gauge to Berrien Springs, and then transferred to the steamer "Twilight" for the river trip to St. Joseph. Both the Buchanan and Berrien Springs bands went along on these all-day outings. It was common for local persons to take the train to Berrien Springs, catch the steamer "May Graham" for the ride down the St. Joseph River to St. Joseph, and take a lake boat from there to Chicago. Because of its winding route along the river, the rail route came to be known locally as "The Pumpkin Vine".

Plans to extend the railroad to St. Joseph on the north and to South Bend to the south never materialized. A new owner took over the considerable mortgages, took up the narrow tracks and installed wide ones, and reached St. Joseph with the railroad before his own financial collapse (which also put two county banks out of business). After this last of a series of financial setbacks, the railroad was taken over by the Pere Marquette line and was finally abandoned in the early 1900's. But for 20 years the riverside Narrow Gauge had provided excitement, (such as the time in 1882 the train made the run from Berrien Springs in 22 minutes, "making the crew's hair stand on end") and for 20 years the ill-starred conveyance had helped fill the social calendars of Buchanan.

"Old Fort Sumpter"

In the midst of all the Victorian era and gay 90's social whirl in Buchanan, affairs of more serious nature were taking place in the growing town.

In 1860, the Buchanan Union School (the Dewey Avenue school) had graduated its first class. The graduation program, called then a School Exhibition, had featured recitations by the graduates...all boys. Later, the first graduating class at the new high school consisted of all girls.

Construction of the new high school on Chicago Street (in the building now housing part of the high school trade school shop) was underway in 1871; and was completed at a cost of $38,000. Students were transferred to the new school in September, 1872. The new school, dubbed "Old Fort Sumpter" by the townsfolk, was a combined grade and high school. The first four-year high school class was graduated in 1877, consisting of Lillie B. Howe, Emma Smith, Fannie Woodworth, Nettie Bainton, and Minnie Hamilton.

Smoke Eaters of the Past

Firefighting in the formative years of old Buchanan was a serious and almost hopeless task, once the "destroying element" had gotten started in the closely spaced wood frame building of the village. Fire brigades, using collapsible leather buckets hung for the purpose near the door of every store and factory, offered the only hope; and even with every man, woman and child lined up in a bucket brigade from McCoy's Creek to the scene of the fire, little could be done to save even the smallest shed. Every mill along the creek was at last totally destroyed by fire, except the present Co-ops mill, which itself was once partially burned.

After the disastrous fire of 1862 which destroyed nearly all the buildings downtown, steps were taken to secure better fire protection. A. Willard was appointed first fire chief of the village; and he purchased for the town the first fire-fighting equipment, a Button hand-pumper, put into use here in 1867. By 1873, Willard had organized an engine company and a hose company. Some years later, there were three companies, including a hook and ladder company, (but no hook and ladder truck) with a total membership of 50 men. The first fire-fighting company was called the Saratoga Fire Company No. 1 of the Village of Buchanan. In the early 80's, the department agitated for the purpose of a steam fire engine; and in 1884 the common council purchased a Silsby steam engine at a cost of $4,000. About 1910, the town acquired a Ford chemical truck.

The large fire companies of the 70's and 80's were a social institution of the first order, sporting flashy uniforms, appearing in every kind of parade, and staging firemen's balls and picnic excursions that were invariably the festive highlight of the season. In 1889 the Alert Hose Company was formed; and it was from this prestigious group that a team of fleet-footed athletes was drawn to uphold the laurels of Buchanan in the hose cart race tournaments held in Niles, Michigan City, and neighboring towns.

The fire fighters of early days enjoyed the same kind of hero worship accorded the Buchanan Blues, an independent baseball team that was "the scourge of southwestern Michigan" in the 90's.

Chapter Ten

FROM BROAD AXE TO DYNAMO IN McCOY LAND

If some curious archaeologist many thousands of years from now should decide to dig (with molecular eradication rays, of course...not a primitive shovel) into the likely looking basin between low southern hills and the wide curve of an ancient river, he might discover near the uppermost earth strata the evidence of the town of Buchanan, and by careful analysis of his artifacts reconstruct the progression of the past civilization thusly:

The Flintlock and Hand Tool Age, the Waterwheel and Small-Shop Age, the Wooden Age, and the Iron and Fabricated Steel Age. There might even be evidence of a Laser-Atomic Age to crown the future scientist's findings.

Or, if you prefer simple facts to such flighty, time-machine jargon, let us just say that there have been in Buchanan's history some very definite periods of concentrated industry to mark the advancing decades.

Although the growth of this city may not be unique in the annals of the overall rise of America, the story of how Buchanan ran the entire gamut of manufacturing methods and power from hand to the electric motor, covering the entire development of modern manufacture is, to us at least, a fascinating part of our heritage. Even more intriguing is the exploration of the fateful circumstances...and mere caprices of nature...which on several occasions saved the town from becoming a "has-been".

In addition to the kind "caprice of nature" which put McCoy's Creek in a handsome and fertile valley to begin with, some of these fateful circumstances included the nearby priceless timberlands, the unexpected coming of the railroad through the town, the coming of electric power just as the timber ran out...and even the faraway San Francisco earthquake which, had it occurred a day earlier, would likely have cost Buchanan its huge Clark Equipment Company. All of these factors have been or will be explored in this saga of "The Real McCoy".

Water Wheel to Turbine Wheel

The small-shop and mill era, from 1834 to 1860, provided the fundamental needs of the settlers. The Wooden Age, when the town predominated as a furniture and wagon-making center, lasted from approximately 1860 to 1890. The Iron Age, from 1894 to the present, began with a first small steel fabrication plant in Buchanan...which took root and grew into a large industry.

The marked ages in industrial development here logically coincided with the advancement of power sources. Water power prevailed until the late 1870's; and steam power, introduced in the late 60's, became the main source of power from 1880 to 1894, when electricity became available in Buchanan.

Buchanan Industries in the Eighties

In a previous chapter, we listed the local business establishments as recorded in 1873. Ten years later, in 1883, the Berrien County Record reported, in addition to the flour and saw mills: four wholesale furniture factories, the Zinc Collar Pad Factory, two spring bed factories, a cabinet organ factory, two carriage factories, two wagon shops, a foundry, machine shop, six blacksmith shops, three harness shops, two cooper shops, and thirteen dressmaking establishments.

At one time, four carpet-stretcher factories were claimed for Buchanan; and in the 80's, the Hatch Cutlery Works was reported to be the largest employer. In the late 70's and early 80's, the four furniture manufacturers totaled an annual output of 100,000 bedsteads, mostly for trade in the West and Southwest (an area just being developed). The need for good cheap furniture prompted the Black and Willard Factory to turn out a bedstead that sold for $1.25, shipped "knocked down" and unpainted to Kansas City. Jenny Lind beds and trundle beds were also their specialty...also many designs with fine scrollwork made from original designs.

Another furniture factory, the Buchanan Manufacturing Company, annually used 1,200,000 board feet of selected walnut, maple, ash, poplar, and linden, of which the Buchanan district grew the finest in America. Oak and hickory were commonly used in the making of carriages and wagons. The Buchanan Manufacturing Company also tried for a while the making of the briefly sensational "Queen Folding Bed"; and the George Black Factory for a period of years turned out the "Queen of the West" garden plow. Much excelsior was made and sold as a by-product of the wood industries.

An indication of the "boom" in Buchanan was noted in the Record when on February 3, 1881, J.D. Ross, the local banker, counted 150 teams in the business section at one time in the middle of the afternoon and estimated that 400 teams came to town that day.

The Bainton Mill

The wood-working shops of the 70's and 80's were not the only source of job opportunities attracting people to Buchanan. The afore-mentioned volume-producing flour and grist mills were also doing a thriving business, as was a large mill not yet mentioned.

Kelsey Bainton, a Buchanan native, has provided a first-hand account, taken from memory and from family records, of the big, picturesque Bainton...or Niagara...Mill, which was a Buchanan landmark for many years.

Charles Lincoln Bainton (father of Kelsey) and William Franklin Bainton were very young boys when their father, William, died in 1865. The elder Bainton, a native of Yorkshire, England, had build the McCoy's Creek mill race and a grist mill, the forerunner of the present Co-ops mill. This early family venture was told in an earlier chapter. As young men the brothers, heirs to the large Bainton farm now covered by the main plant of Clark Equipment Company, determined to carry on the family trade as millers. They leased and managed the grist mill at Dayton for some time; and later, when the Black and Willard Furniture Factory was moved into the former Floral Hall and Rink structures (also located on the former Bainton estate) they built their own mill at the former site of the furniture factory, using the water falls at the downstream end of the Bainton Mill Pond on McCoy's Creek.

The Bainton mill, producer of the widely known Niagara Flour, was powered by a unique method designed to increase the applied force of the creek. In this method, a second waterfall was built some distance downstream from the mill; and power produced by this falls was transmitted upstream by a device described by Kelsey Bainton as an "endless rope". The device operated on the chain-drive principle, using water wheel, pulleys, and heavy rope.

The power system employed by the Bainton mill is shown in a large oil painting made around the turn of the century by Kelsey's mother, Mrs. Charles (Amy) Bainton. The oil painting is now a treasured family heirloom in the Bainton home.

In the early 20th century, the Bainton brothers also opened a grocery store in downtown Buchanan; and Niagara Flour was a featured item in the store. In 1924, however, the Bainton mill finally met the fate to which other local mills had earlier succumbed, being completely destroyed by fire. The costly, spectacular Bainton mill fire is still remembered by long-time Buchanan residents.

End of an Era

More suddenly than it had arrived, the great Wooden Age in Buchanan came to a more-or-less unforeseen end; and by about 1889 most of the singing rotary saws in the wood-fragrant shops and factories had, one by one, ground to a wheezing halt.

A few factories continued, with curtailed production, for a number of years; but boastful reports of 30 cars of furniture shipped weekly...23,000 hatracks and 1,650 center tables annually...1,000 looking glass frames, 100,000 bedsteads, 3,500 lounges, and other wooded products numbering in the thousands, had ceased. Such volume had finally produced the inevitable dilemma, depletion of the timberlands in the area. Logging crews were ranging farther and farther westward as the great Galien Woods receded, until it was no longer feasible to haul the lumber such great distances.

Some local factories had been importing materials at reduced profit for some time, as illustrated in a Chicago Times article written in 1883, describing an exhibit of "the finest display of wagons at the Illinois State Fair".

Said the Times, "These wagons are manufactured by the Rough Brothers Wagon Works, Buchanan, Michigan. Six wagons are on exhibit. One is a common stock wagon; one with dark wine-colored body and straw-colored gearings, elegantly decorated; another two bodies are of white walnut, oiled and polished, revealing the beauty of the texture and grain. The sides of one are beautifully and richly decorated in Japanese designs of gold, ivory, and color, executed by hand and displaying exceedingly fine taste and artistic skill. The axle trees are of Ohio hickory; the hubs of Pennsylvania black birch; the spokes and felloes of Indiana Oak."

As production in Buchanan fell off with the scarcity of local materials, the market void was filled by manufacturers in other Michigan towns and in other states having good timber supplies and easy transportation; and Buchanan faced the seemingly inevitable fate of becoming a "saw-mill ghost town."

That this did not indeed happen was due in large part to one of those "fateful circumstances" mentioned earlier...an accident of fate personified in an heroic and crusading editor of the Berrien County Record who saw a great, untapped source of prosperity and salvation for the town, and proceeded to put his dreams into action.

In doing so, he was to lose his own fortune and commit little McCoy's Creek forever to a grave of concrete and lost glory.

Chapter Eleven

ELECTRICITY... A FIERY EDITOR'S CRUSADE

Today, in an age of expanding businesses, newly created jobs, and fluctuating economy, names and faces in Buchanan are apt to change from year to year.

Such was not the case in this town's first hundred years...before World War II, say...for in those years the town moved along at a slower pace, in an intimate state of everyone-knowing-everyone, if only by name.

Yet today, many of the long-familiar family names in the Buchanan area are carried on in the progeny of men who built the town...those ancestors whose genius mortared the structure of the growing city and whose contributions may be perpetuated in the names of streets, roads, area lakes, schools, and town additions.

One whose name must rank high in the list of illustrious pioneers is that of John G. Holmes, a man of vision and perserverance who gave the town a new surge of life just as it threatened to die with the old century.

Many years after his crackling, 19-year stint as owner, publisher, and editor of the Berrien County Record, Buchanan's legacy from John G. Holmes was recalled by a later editor who wrote, "He (John Holmes) enlightened the citizens, lighted the town, and lightened his pocketbook".

Buchanan was riding high on a wave of prosperity when the fiery Holmes took over the Record in 1875. Amid the heavy creak of lumber wagons in the streets, the lusty screech of sawmills, the impatient whistle of loaded freight trains straining westward...Editor Holmes sat quietly at his desk and with sharpened pencil began a 20-year crusade to lead the town in a better direction than the one it was then heading.

That he finally succeeded, at a time when the town was teetering on the brink of economic oblivion nearly 18 years later, constitutes a most interesting chapter of our history...a chapter marked by the rising roar of the electric motor, and the dying murmur of "The Real McCoy."

We can follow the course of those years through Holmes' own writings.

In the mid-seventies Holmes, new to the job, caustically remarked in an editorial that cows left roaming the streets at night "should at least have the bells taken off"; and sometime later he wrote that "Days Avenue has at last been graded and crowned with gutters at the sides, but the work is being spoiled by the rootings of the village swine."

In May, 1878, Holmes sounded the first trumpet of a long, personal campaign when he noted that the town had only one street light...and that in front of the post office, costing three cents a day in kerosene. Three years later he reported only five town street lights, and stated that there should be 40 such lights.

Then in January, 1880, with carefully veiled enthusiasm the editor remarked, "Since the announcement of Edison's success with the electric light (in 1879) we are not in so great a hurry for kerosene lamps on our streets, but are willing to wait until we hear of the success of this invention, and, if within reach, we shall ask for a few of those lamps."

That was the year that the town's pine walks, laid in 1865, were giving out, and were replaced with walks of brick and "black concrete". And in 1883, after a series of outcries in the press concerning the "sinkholes of the town", the cement culvert over McCoy's Creek at the intersection of Days and Front streets was completed.

Ignoring the progressive editor's plea for "a few of those lamps", however, Buchanan in 1887 replaced the town's kerosene lamps with 50 gasoline lights.

Undaunted by such setbacks the stubborn Holmes, seeing that the town was facing a crisis with the depletion of the timberlands supplying the thriving furniture and wagon factories, drummed continuously on the prospects for new manufacturing here if foresighted citizens would "get the jump" on neighboring towns along the river by building a dam across the river to generate electric power. His pleas fell on deaf ears, for the most part.

A serious local depression descended on Buchanan with the closing of the wood manufacturing companies in the early 1900's; and the spirit and financial means of any possible "foresighted citizens" simultaneously departed.

At last Holmes determined, after 13 years of pleading his cause, to follow his own advice. Already involved in platting an addition to the town through the firm of Holmes and English, Holmes engineered an enlargement of the firm which on April 4, 1893, became the corporation of Buchanan Power and Electric Company. Officers included Peter English, Frank English, A.J. Carothers, John G. Holmes, and Enos Holmes.

Mortgaging all their assets, the partners hired a crew and began work on the dam June 15, 1893. The wooden structure was completed in September of that same year; and as the water of the mighty St. Joseph crept upward against the timbers, a crowd of 600 persons gathered along the banks to watch as the structure held, and the water surged over the top. (Fifteen years later, the dam washed out, and was replaced in stone and concrete by later owners.)

Doubting Thomases

During the years of Holmes' campaign, his slogan had been "Dam the river and boom the town"; and during actual construction his opponents, of which there were many, turned the phrase around to read, "Boom the river and damn the town!" (A "boom", in river log-rafting days was a heavy timber which served to hold in check the floating logs.)

Skepticism in the town continued as work was begun on a power plant designed to generate enough electricity to furnish 1200 incandescent and 52 arc lamps, plus 250 horsepower for manufacturing.

Doubters were by no means convinced, even as the work of setting poles and stringing lights began. One of the elder residents was reported to have remarked to an appreciative audience on a downtown street corner that there seemed to be something wrong with the wire...there was no hole in it for the light to go through.

January 4, 1894, the dynamos started; and January 17, the lights were lit for the first time in a test section of downtown Buchanan. The city fathers and the townsfolk were then caught up in the spirit of the phenomenon of electric power and the streets were crowded, with the Buchanan Band Boys turned out to play for the occasion.

Back at his desk at the Record, Holmes, allowing himself a moment of careful jubilation wrote, "The improvement over kerosene and gasoline lamps is very noticeable. With electric lights...and a first-class system of waterworks which must follow...Buchanan is strictly in it!"

Of course, the Record became the first enterprise in Buchanan to make use of electric power to operate its machinery; and the issue of February 15, 1894, declared in bold type: "Printed by the St. Joseph River...believe it or not!"

Very soon, the town installed its first municipal water works system, using power-driven pumps. (Until then, the nearest thing to a public waterworks system had been the old "Jacob's Well" on Front Street just west of the present Buchanan Public Library at the George Black residence, where persons with malfunctioning wells of their own came to fill their buckets.)

Town Wins--Holmes Loses

Unfortunately, the Buchanan Power and Electric Company was organized by Publisher Holmes just as the country was in the throes of an overall financial panic; and the Holmes and English corporation was mortgaged "to the hilt" by the time work on the dam and power plant was completed.

Before any real profit could be counted, or any financial salvation found, forclosure proceedings were started by the mortgage holder, Fred Lee of Dowagiac.

Lee, who had married the daughter of P.D. Beckwith, founder and builder of the Round Oak Stove Works, was then president of that company, and was considered a millionaire in financial circles. When the court had completed foreclosure on the Buchanan Dam, the structure and accruing property were deeded to Fred and Kate Lee. (Later, in 1900, the Lees sold the dam to Charles A. Chapin, while reserving two acres at the site of the Lee & Porter Axle Works, and the rights to the first 125 horsepower generated by the river.)

To settle his debts, Holmes was forced to sell the Record in 1894. The crusading editor of the 19th century was able to see his dream for Buchanan come true through his own heroic initiative, and to witness the beginnings of modern manufacturing here, while losing his own material wealth in the process. He did indeed, "dam the river and boom the town"..."getting the jump", as he had envisioned, on any other community in the area, and achieving the coup of luring new business to Buchanan with the promise of cheap electric power.

And so it was that the roar of the dynamos down on the river, not far downstream from where little McCoy's Creek joined the mightier current, signaled the beginnings of a new era in Buchanan.

Chapter Twelve

NEW INDUSTRY AND A NEW CENTURY

Fred Lee, wealthy, sagacious businessman from Dowagiac, knew a good opportunity when he saw it.

In 1893, the Round Oak Stove Company president turned a willing ear, a speculative eye, and his financial resources toward Buchanan, sharing with John G. Holmes a vision of new industrial growth for this riverside town. After providing the financial means for the building of the electric power dam at Buchanan, Lee acted at once to make use, himself, of the new power source for manufacturing. In so doing, he led the way into a new era of industry in the faltering community which had been within a hair's breadth of becoming an economic ghost town.

Two years before his acquisition of the St. Joseph River power dam through mortgage foreclosure, Lee formed a partnership with another Dowagiac man, Henry Porter, and began to set up a factory here.

As a huge sign on their factory later proclaimed, Porter held patents for: Porter's Patent Dust-Proof Axles, Porter's Patent Ball-Bearing Axles, Porter's Patent Wood Rim Wire Wheels for Solid and Pneumatic Rubber Tires and Famous Pan-American Gear.

Lee extended his interests in Buchanan when in 1897 he opened the Lee Brothers Bank here in partnership with his father Chauncey and brother Henry. For 35 years he maintained investments in Buchanan, including ownership of the Lee Hotel (Hotel Rex) and a half-dozen other buildings in the business section.

Lee & Porter Axles

The building of the axle works was begun in 1894 with the erection of the first factory unit on the near river bluff above the new dam. A Michigan Central spur line, two miles long, was laid along the eastern outskirts of town, crossing the Rynearson and Niles-Buchanan roads, bridging McCoy's Creek near its mouth, and ending in an embankment at the downstream end of the long axle works complex.

The Lee & Porter factory started production in the making of carriage axles in 1895, with a force of 50 men and a payroll of $2,500.

Almost immediately, the company was able to establish an extensive export business, shipping "L & P Axles" to Australia, New Zealand, and South Africa.

A unique product made and exported by Lee & Porter was a wire-spoked, pneumatic-tired "Bike Wheel" shipped to the Orient (India and China) for use on the man-powered rickshaws (or rickshas), an Eastern, two-wheeled version of the taxicab.

Another product eventually used over a wide area was the heavy steel axle made for the Concord Coach Factory of Massachusetts. Concord Coaches had played a distinguished part in the history of American transportation...their leather-hung, enclosed bodies lurching over the frontier trails for nearly a century. While the stage is now considered a pre-railway vehicle, it was in fact used as an adjunct to the railways until well into the 20th century; and thus many of the famous old stages were carried on Lee & Porter axles during the last 10 years of their operation.

Considering the export trade carried on by the young but booming company, it also seems likely that those axles traveled not only along the remote trails of the West, but across the veldts through the African gold and diamond mining country, and across the Australian bush country, as well. It would no doubt be a gross...but pleasant...exaggeration to say that, at the turn of the century, the world turned on Lee & Porter axles.

Among the earliest employees at Lee & Porter, during the days of carriage axle production, were Charles Dumbolton, Charles Simpson, Morrow Chubb, Judson Markham, J.L. Vincent, Guy Young, Walter Hathaway, Cap Ashby, Henry Eisele, Peter Bachman, Charles Koons, Judd Clary (secretary-treasurer of the company), George Bennitt, Herb Hanover, George Ditto, and Arthur Voorhees.

After several years of wagon axle production, the company found itself on the brink of a new industry when R.J. Burrows came to the Buchanan plant in 1909 to work on his plans for automobile axles. The success of this new venture coincided with the growing demand for "gas buggy" axles; and before long the plant was able to discontinue its wire wheel production and concentrate on this auto parts manufacture. (Burrows later became a moving force in the Clark Equipment Company, after the automotive division of the burned-out Lee & Porter plant was absorbed by the forerunner of Clark in 1913. He served as a Clark vice president from 1917 to 1947).

And so it was that progress and production change in the Lee & Porter factory marked the break from the horse and buggy era to the automotive age. The axle works in Buchanan was the forerunner of the modern machine shops and, as events proved, the embryo of the automotive department of Clark Equipment Company.

Fire in Buchanan...Again

Not long after midnight February 11, 1913, Buchanan people were aroused by a sinister glow at the northeast edge of town, and before the horse-drawn hook and ladder truck and the hose cart could plow through huge snow drifts to the Lee & Porter factory, the fire, driven by high winds in the bitter night, had raced along oil-soaked floors and sped upward in an all-consuming conflagration. All that was saved were a few charred blueprints.

Later temporary quarters were set up in the old "Beehive" building on Days Avenue, where E.C. Mogford, the plant draughtsman, labored for weeks to reconstruct lost blueprints. But the salvage work proved puny indeed in the face of the fact that the fire had ended the story of Buchanan's first machine shop, had consumed $300,000 worth of machinery in the automotive axle department alone, and had burned 130 men out of a job.

George Rich Company

Our story here goes back to 1903, when, in a Canal Street basement workshop in Chicago, George Rich read an advertisement in a Chicago paper offering cheap electric power and facilities for manufacturing in Buchanan, Michigan. Rich had just developed a revolutionary steel drill, and was looking for a machine shop location with a ready labor market and the other assets offered by Buchanan. In 1904, he set up his shop on Main Street, in the former Rough Wagon Works building, and started production..."on a shoestring".

There were then only three industries in Buchanan: The Buchanan Cabinet Company, the Lee & Porter Axle Works, and the Zinc Collar Pad Company.

At the beginning of this century, the railroads were undoubtedly the biggest business in America, reaching out with steel fingers across the prairie lands and mountains to tie the seas together. Railway equipment plants then used flat carbon-steel drills to pierce the steel rails, but...it was commonly remarked...if one started on Monday morning to drill through inch-thick malleable iron, he could expect to see light through it sometime Thursday.

The George Rich Manufacturing Company revolutionized the drilling process by making the first twisted steel drill, which worked as a carpenter's bit, cleaning the hole it made.

(Here, this writer is compelled to insert a qualification. In compiling any history, an author is often faced with contradictions in records; and in this case, one research source credited George Rich, not with the invention of the famous Celfor Drill, but "a boring bar with an eccentric sleeve". Exhaustive inquiries have failed to turn up the truth of the matter, a distinction which might be of some importance to the pioneer men of Clark Equipment Company.)

The product eventually found a tremendous market; but in its tottering infancy the company lived and produced only from day to day, nearly collapsing more than once from financial starvation.

There is one story...not verified by this writer, but intriguing in its implications in the story of Buchanan...suggesting that, had the San Francisco earthquake occurred a day earlier, the Clark Equipment Company would never have been born.

One of the George Rich Company's best customers was in San Francisco. When the great earthquake hit on April 18, 1906, so the story goes, the California company was buried beyond recovery under debris of the quake, along with a large shipment of tools for which the Buchanan shop had not received payment. When news of the disaster was heard in Buchanan, it seemed that the local firm might as well have been buried in the quake, for the payment was necessary to meet the payroll and buy raw material to continue operation. Several days later, however, a bank draft for the tools came through from the west coast firm. It had been issued and sent out the day before the earthquake.

In the year after the San Francisco earthquake, the high-speed twist drill brought prosperity to the Rich Manufacturing Company, along with a new name and a new owner and president.

Celfor Tool Company

Eugene B. Clark, an 1894 graduate of the engineering department of Cornell University, had been employed for 11 years as assistant manager of the Illinois Steel Company (employing 10,000 men) before casting his fate with the small machine shop in Buchanan. He purchased the George Rich Manufacturing Company in 1907, the same year it became Celfor Tool. The new name was of Latin origin, taken from "celeritas", meaning speed, and "fortis", strength.

Operations were moved to new buildings erected for the company by the town (now a part of the Clark complex) which were later purchased by the company.

Expansion thereafter was rapid, and Celfor Tools, including boring bars and sockets, drills and reamers, were soon in wide demand.

Among the early directors who contributed their energies and wisdom to the building of the company was M.L. Hanlin, who served as general manager from 1905 (when there were 17 employees) to 1917, and then as vice president and manager of the tool division of Clark until 1947. The late Mr. Hanlin was also mayor of Buchanan and president of the school board for many years. (He also organized the Clark Players, an active and highly acclaimed dramatic group whose performances in the Clark Theatre and elsewhere were legend until their disbandment during World War II).

Edwin B. Ross, who later became a Clark vice president, came to Buchanan with the formation of the Buchanan Electric Steel Manufacturing Company in 1911, which was organized to produce high-speed alloy steel for drills. This company (BESCO) installed and used in its steel production a huge electric steel furnace, one of the first in America. Later the company purchased the Peerless Crucible Steel Castings Company of Detroit to provide its alloy steels, and the new plant in Buchanan was converted to a foundry.

It All Becomes Clark

Before World War I, Celfor Tool Company was making cast-steel wheels for trucks, an internal gear drive axle, and a front steering axle, in addition to the drills and other Celfor Tools.

Separate enterprizes were then merged into a single, all-encompassing manufacturing organization which on December 27, 1916, became the Clark Equipment Company.

Early employees not yet mentioned (before the formation of Clark Equipment Company) who later rose to prominent positions as officers and directors in the giant organization included: Frank Habicht, who joined Celfor Tool in 1908, became a Clark vice president, and served more than 42 years on the board of directors; E.C. Mogford, Lester Lyon, K.K. Knapp, and Albert Bonner, who succeeded E.B. Clark as company president in 1942.

In the years ahead, after 1916, Clark's variety of products, its volume of production, and its markets were to mushroom, bringing worldwide recognition to the Clark name...and, by association, to Buchanan, Michigan...a little town with a "big daddy" industry...and a small creek which was occasionally useful for church baptisms, gathering watercress, washing milk cans, and cooling off small boys after school.

Chapter Thirteen

BUCHANAN...A CITY OF THE TWENTIETH CENTURY

At the turn of the century, Buchanan was a town of 1,708 citizens whose lives were more or less regulated by the rooster's crow, the school bell, the train whistle, the church bell, and the shop whistle.

The town's aspect was one of serenity and neighborliness. Dirt streets, graced by soft canopies of overhanging elms, led outward in narrowing tracks to the wheat fields, rolling pasture land, and country apple orchards whose fragrance on still spring evenings reached the sociable, wrap-around porches up and down Front Street. Red brick and gray-painted frame houses, some three stories high and with leaded, color-paned front doors and brass pull-bells, were set in yards deep enough to accommodate the summer house, the woodshed, the out house, and a barn for the buggy, the cutter, and old Dobbin. Here, between the kitchen door and the barn one might find a latticed grape or rose arbor, the chicken yard, a patch of rhubarb, and a rope swing dangling from a black walnut tree.

Footpaths, where there were no streets, led kitty-corner across open fields to outlying houses, to the river, to the mills and factories, to the school, and to the best fishing and wading places along McCoy's Creek.

Downtown, large proud buildings of imported brick with arched windows like raised eyebrows were forced to look down upon tar-roofed, gray-slatted neighbors whose meager interiors dispensed pickles and flour from barrels, boiling beef and headcheese, dress lengths and curled-feather bonnets, liniment and horehound drops, and sarsaparillas on Saturday afternoons. Hitching rails were everywhere; and a large, round horse-watering basin stood near the corner on Days Avenue next to the hotel.

The "Gas Buggies"

The coming of the Michigan Motor and Machine Company to Buchanan from Detroit in 1904, for the purpose of building automobiles, did not offer any lasting threat to the livery businesses of Ed McCollum, Ed Bird, Will House, Curley Uplinger, or George Batchelor, although for a time, reading the gleeful headlines by the current Record editor, townsfolk were led to believe Buchanan rather than Detroit would become the automotive center of the world. The company produced two automobiles before its demise...; the first, a combination carry all and dray for Will House, and a second model for Myron S. Mead. Two other early autos also provided more conversation than transportation on Buchanan streets...a two-cylindered Apperson, made in Indianapolis and owned by Henry Porter of Lee & Porter Axle Works, and a steam Locomobile owned by Tom Brown, a foreman at the same plant.

In 1912, Harry Boyce opened the town's first garage and auto agency in the old "Beehive" building on Days Avenue, site of the former skating rink, and here he sold his first Ford to Ed McCollum.

Clark Brings Population Boom

Between the years 1910 and 1920, Buchanan's population gained more than at any other time in this century to date, going from 1,831 in 1910 to 3,187 in 1920, according to official census figures. The second largest population gain was recorded during the years of World War II, with a count of 4,056 persons in 1940, and 5,224 in 1950. The rise during each of those decades can be attributed to a corresponding growth of production and markets within the Clark Equipment Company.

In a belated effort to catch up to its own progress, the town in 1922 built a new, large high school and elementary school (the present Buchanan High School) in front of the former school building on Chicago Street. The earlier school, which had been built in 1870 (and which had used kerosene lamps for lighting until 1918) was then converted into a heating plant and school shop quarters.

Buchanan was chartered as a city in 1935.

The Clark Equipment Company, meanwhile, had continued to advance in technology, adding new products and expanding its markets. The years of World War I had brought orders by the thousands for axles and wheels. This period also brought a new industry to the American scene when Clark built the first materials handling truck for moving heavy loads in its own plant. Clark called the new vehicle the Trucktractor. Early models carried dump bodies; later ones held lifting platforms, forks, and crane hooks. Visitors to the plant were highly impressed with these industrial carriers, and orders began pouring in. Clark, having outgrown the capacity of the Buchanan plant, built a Trucktractor plant in Battle Creek.

A decade later, Clark had expanded operations by starting manufacture of truck transmissions, and this successful venture again entailed new facilities. In 1928, the company acquired the Frost Gear and Forge Company of Jackson, to provide a source for gears and shafts. A Clark transmission assembly plant was built in Berrien Springs in 1930. Finally, in 1950, all transmission manufacturing was consolidated in a new factory in Jackson.

Clark's variety of products continued to mushroom, and it started making one-piece forged axle housings in 1929. The AutoTram, a pioneer aluminum streamlined train, was shown at the Chicago Century of Progress Exhibition in 1933; and the company in 1934 developed railway-car trucks that operated quietly thru hypoid gears. In that same year the company introduced "blind" rivets...metal fasteners that could be placed from one side only, along with a pneumatic "gun" for setting them.

Clark's production of axle housings and transmissions for Army trucks boomed during World War II, as well as the demand for fork trucks and heavy towing tractors. Buchanan servicemen ,arriving at huge bases and tiny landing-strip atolls in every corner of the world could feel a moment of kinship with home at sight of the weird-looking "bugs", with the Clark name, towing out swept-wing fighters and scooting around under huge bombers, moving supplies and materiel.

Today, Clark maintains a world-wide dealer organization, Clark International, to meet the ever-increasing demand for its products in the materials handling industry.

Other Industries

A plating works, Larson Steel Products, was organized by Daniel Larson in 1931; and in 1935, under the leadership of Elmer Cress, the company was reorganized and became Buchanan Steel Products. With the installation of several drop forge hammers, the company enjoyed a steady growth, and in 1964 was merged with National Standard Company of Niles. The Buchanan plant presently employs 250 persons.

Electro-Voice, Inc., headed by Albert Kahn, moved to Buchanan in 1946. Beginning with the production of microphones for the electronic communications industry, the company expanded steadily with the added production of electric organs, electronic amplifiers, speakers, and component parts. The company is now a subsidiary of Gulton Industries, Inc.

Additional manufacturers of Buchanan in 1975 included, with the date of their establishment: Buchanan Metalform, Incorporated, Division of Excel Corporation, 1965; Carbon's Malted Flour, 1930; C & S Corporation, 1966; Industrial Machine Works, Incorporated, 1953; Jemco, Incorporated, 1964; Pride Pattern and Manufacturing, Incorporated, 1970; White Welder Company, 1959; FAPCO, 1969; Pinlock Engineering, 1970; H.S. Cover Company, 1972.

McCoy's Creek Forgotten

The reader may perhaps be aware that this story no longer matches its title...that the story of McCoy's Creek has fallen by the wayside in this accelerated chronicle of Buchanan in the 20th century.

That's just the way it was with McCoy's Creek. Once the roots of modern industry had taken hold, the creaking and sloshing of the old water wheels up and down the stream was all but forgotten in the prosperous roar of dynamos, electric furnaces, and giant machines.

The Bainton Flour mill continued in the old tradition until it burned down in 1924; and the large mill pond was then filled in and covered over by an expanding Clark Equipment Company.

In the 1920's, local citizens dredged out an area near the headgates on the city land down behind the high school to make a pleasant swimming pond for the young people of the town, but the unfinished project faltered with the waning days of summer. The lasting result of the project was that the dam and control gates at the creek's dividing point crumbled away, reducing the flow in the mill race and allowing the buildup of silt and weeds.

Water power developed in the mill race was used until 1945 to operate a corn-cracking unit in the basement of the Buchanan Co-ops Mill, but this practice was finally abandoned because the variability of the flow in the race made the power undependable.

End of Water Power

The abandonment of the water-powered turbine in the Co-ops mill marked the finale of more than a century of direct use of water power for manufacturing in Buchanan.

Several attempts were made over the years to preserve McCoy's Creek in its natural beauty as much as possible. In 1945, a meeting of property owners along the mill race was held in the city hall to decide the fate of the raceway. Many wished to dredge out and clean up the stream to restore the waterway to its former glory. A few wished to close off and abandon the mill race, dividing the property among the adjacent owners; but a tangle of controversy over property lines left the question unresolved, and stirred up a torrent of protests from citizens over the mere thought of destroying the potentially beautiful waterway.

Letters-to-the-editor poured in. Rol S. Black, born in Buchanan in 1880, spoke for many when he wrote, "The old raceway was a thing of beauty and an asset to Buchanan for nearly a hundred years, and could again be a thing of beauty if it were cleaned up, all dumping prohibited, sightly dams created at the headgates, a portion of the creek diverted into the race so that it would become a clear-running stream again. Pathways along both banks with a row of trees behind them. Then, since the water power at the end of the flume is to be abandoned, why not put in some permanent concrete work with a cascading waterfall in downtown Buchanan? People come to this country and drive miles to look at some falling water in a stream no larger than McCoy's Creek." The letter, and others like it, were written in 1945.

As the town grew and modernized, it became expedient to extend the widening streets, the foundations of buildings, and the concrete of parking lots over the downtown portion of the creek...and it became in fact an expensive, as well as engineering, nuisance to channel the perpetually willful and exuberant waters of the stream into the large, dark tubes which permitted the leveling of the ground and the orderly development and refinement (?) of the town.

But it was accomplished.

THRESHING TIME . . . Near the turn of the century, near Buchanan.

Epilogue

THE REAL McCOY ... HAS BEEN ... IS ... TO BE?

Back in 1904, the editor of the Berrien County Record, pleased with nearly a century of progress in Buchanan and momentarily caught up in the imminent prospects for its industrial rebirth, foretold its future in bold type:

SPLENDID PROSPECTS IN VIEW FOR BUCHANAN.
EVERYTHING IS THRIVING. THIS IS A BEAUTIFUL TOWN.

More than 70 years have now passed since those jubilant headlines, years in which the town, for the most part, has lived up to its press notices of 1904.

Bolstered by its many natural assets, set firmly within an ever-growing industrial belt that stretches from New England to Chicago, encircled by an expanding network of interstate expressways, the still-small city has more than held its own in today's fast-paced world. New industries have been added...and some few subtracted. New schools have been built to serve all neighborhoods, and modern churches have replaced the old. Stylized apartment complexes within the city reflect the housing changes of the past decade; and today Buchanan can even boast of lovely suburbs with quaintly-named, winding streets, pushing back the farm fields.

In 1974, Clark Equipment Company moved its corporate headquarters into a magnificent new building of glass, steel, and stone at the north edge of the city, on a bluff where once the women of Chief Moccasin's village may have watched the river for the returning canoes of their hunters.

Today, Buchanan has achieved an enviable position which allows it to function successfully in a cosmopolitan milieu, while yet retaining much of the charm and beauty of "the old home town". Any true-blue Buchananite would proclaim this "the best of both worlds".

And what of McCoy's Creek?

As noted in the last chapter, the waterway that had served as the genesis for the town was all but forgotten in the acceleration of the 20th century...sacrificed to modernization and expansion, and the bulldozer.

This is not to say that it was unused! It was indeed used freely, for many years, as a convenient dumping ground for industrial waste, cans, old tires, candy wrappers, sewage...all manner of debris and dross of an uncaring citizenry.

It would therefore seem that the very subject of this book, the "hero" of our title, has in the final pages faded away into extinction. Somewhere, between the time in the 19th century when McCoy's Creek was designated "one of the most improved waterways in the state" and the time when the last big water wheel was demolished, this narrative itself forsook the "has-been" stream in tracing the natural course of events, becoming instead a chronicle of progress and growth in a developing community. It had to be.

That being so, are we then left with only some sentimental epitaph for "the old mill stream" before closing the back cover?

A New Look

In a living society, there is always a footnote to history, and here we have a happy one. It can now be reported that between the time the first draft of this history appeared as a series in the Berrien County Record (1967) and the present time, the word "ecology" emerged from the biology classrooms and swept across the country with new meaning; the very word became a rally cry among the people to reverse the long-standing abuses of our environment and natural resources. The message came not only from national conservation groups and tough new federal agencies, but also from concerned local citizen's groups, school children, Scout troops, Lions and Jaycee and Chamber of Commerce, garden clubs and others...not the least of which were conscientious local industries, which have, one by one, taken giant (and often costly) steps to end the pollution of our waterways. And in Buchanan, many hours have been spent by groups of men and boys, thigh-deep in McCoy's Creek with picks, shovels, and rakes, in a mutual endeavor to restore its beauty and cleanliness. In addition, two parks have recently been developed along the stream banks by the city and local organizations.

Another word has come to the fore in America...Heritage! As our country celebrates its Bi-Centennial anniversary of the American Revolution, people everywhere are accelerating their efforts to seek out and preserve and restore the memorablia of yesteryear; and in Buchanan, there are signs that local residents are ready to take a new look at McCoy's Creek and its import upon the community's history.

"History", said President James Garfield, "is but the unrolled scroll of prophesy."

Can it then be mere fantasy to picture a happily-creaking mill wheel once again on McCoy's Creek, perhaps built as a memorial on a yet-undeveloped park site on the lower reaches of the stream? Might there one day be a diversion of the old mill race to a new course down the center of Front Street, with waterfalls and foot bridges to enhance a shaded shopping mall? What new glories might the future hold?

Surely, the final chapter has not been written.

Of one thing we may be fairly certain. As time goes on, the waters of McCoy's Creek will continue to arise from the same perpetual springs at their source and follow their ancient course through Buchanan, dancing by Centennial Park in an everlasting invitation to small boys with fish poles and bare feet. Its gentle cascade will swirl along past shady banks and dappled sunny stretches wherever we allow it.

New generations, even as the old, will pause and lean upon bridge railings to watch and be refreshed, and to ponder for a moment, perhaps, the constant truth and aptness of Alfred, Lord Tennyson's words...written in another day in praise of some other McCoy's Creek...

> "A thousand suns will stream on thee,
> A thousand moons will quiver...
> And here by thee will hum the bee,
> For ever and for ever."

www.ingramcontent.com/pod-product-compliance
Lightning Source LLC
Chambersburg PA
CBHW032017290426
44109CB00013B/696